Cages, Keys
and the
Chatelaine:

A Woman's Book
for Transformation

Arieahn Matamonasa Bennett, Ph.D.

Cages Keys and the Chatelaine:
A woman's book for transformation.
By Arieahn Matamonasa Bennett, Ph.D.

Edited by Waringa Hunja
Cover Design by Rochelle Ratkaj Moser
Front Photo by Kris Downing
Back Photo by Miriam Bulcher

First Edition 2022
Copyright© 2022

Disclaimer

All the information, techniques, skills, and concepts contained within this publication are of the nature of general comment only and are not in any way recommended as individual advice. The intent is to offer a variety of information to provide a wider range of choices now and in the future, recognizing that we all have widely diverse circumstances and viewpoints. Should any reader choose to make use of the information contained herein, this is their decision and the author and publishers do not assume any responsibilities whatsoever under any condition or circumstances.

ISBN: 979-8-9870145-0-9 (Paperback)

Acknowledgments

The ideas for this book started in 2016 while I was teaching a graduate class on navigating life-transitions when doing a lecture on where we get stuck in our lives. At the time I was going to write a short story/allegory tale on a character called "the chatelaine." It was through the encouragement of one of my coaches, Linda Brady that I decided to share so much of my own story. I would especially like to share my heartfelt gratitude for my soul-sister Rhonda Day-Kooy whose constant cajoling kept me working on and finally completing this book. She has been my confidant and cheerleader for decades. I am also eternally grateful for all the women I have worked with in the last two decades whose stories informed and inspired this book.

I am also grateful to my allies and mentors whose powerful coaching and containers created the accountability and inspiration to make this work a priority for completion. I am eternally grateful for all of my mentors who are now in the spirit world: Greg Askenette, Nick Hockings, Don Moccasin, Joe Lancia, and Patricia Monaghan and to all the women in my life who have trusted me to share in their journeys of growth and transformation.

Table of Contents

Preface

I am a cross-culturally trained licensed psychologist, teacher, healer and a leader of women. My soul's purpose is to bring the divine feminine back into balance during this time of upheaval. My work is to create a system for change and liberation based on my experiences with spiritual principles and lessons learned on my own path. It is only now, in my late mid-life, that I recognize I *do* have a system and, if I can teach it to other women, they might experience freedom, joy and lifelong change. What I've realized is that, when women get stuck and are deeply unhappy with our lives, there are common themes and patterns which keep us from reaching their dreams and living an authentic life that we love. The most common culprits are relationships that are highly draining and dysfunctional, patterns of self-abandonment, being instinct-injured and not able to trust ourselves, driven-behavior, overwork and exhaustion and living in a victimhood narrative. In this book, I call these common traps "cages." What I have also discovered in my years of work with women is that there are tools we can learn to use that empower us to gather our energy and power and discover our desires and a new vision for our lives. In this book, I call these "keys." In my own life and in my practice I use journaling as a means for self-knowledge and inner-knowing to assist with identifying the cages, creating a new vision and using the keys as a means for living a balanced, happier life.

I was born to do this work. I was born in the mid-1960s, a time of tumultuous change and social movements. The feminist movement, anti-Vietnam War protests, the environmental movement and the civil rights movement were all gathering momentum. Coming of age in the 1970s had an enormous influence on my worldview and continues to influence the work I do now. Historically, when major cultural paradigms shift, there is always a backlash of the "old guard": those who resist vehemently (and sometimes violently) the changes because they want to cling to the status quo. I believe this is what we are experiencing as a culture right now.

I have been doing this work in a variety of settings and roles throughout my entire adult life, from age 29 to my present late-fifties.While much of my previous written work has been for academic audiences, this book represents a very personal and intimate work of the heart and spirit.

This book is a woman's book, a woman's story. The men in it are significant footnotes in the story; the focus is on the learning that comes from our relationships with them as fathers, brothers, lovers, sons, mentors, friends and sometimes adversaries or enemies. Men's stories have historically overshadowed or erased those of women. We need our own.

I have always believed (and often strongly debated with my male contemporaries) that women experience psychological change and transition differently than men do. For the last several thousand years, women have had to operate in and navigate societies and cultures that are unbalanced and toxic patriarchies. Historically, even when women have been in positions of power, they have ruled at their peril. They often lost their heads and their lives. In a world where power is mainly a male privilege and prerogative, women have had to learn the arts of subtle influence, passive-aggressive communication styles and exercising their dreams, hopes and desires to the best of their ability within the confines and limits of what was culturally acceptable and permissible. When women *do* ascend to leadership roles, we unconsciously co-opt masculine forms of leading in ways that become unhealthy and ultimately unsustainable. Among middle-class and professional women especially, martyrdom and self-sacrifice is a very frequent theme still resonating in the therapy office today. Additionally, for many women, past and present, the development of a type of Stockholm syndrome and/or *learned helplessness* is evident in varying degrees in their therapeutic change narratives. Not only do women have to overcome our own internal wounds, struggles and obstacles, we face numerous social and cultural pathologies as well.

Women in the US and globally face multiple *external* social, economic and cultural obstacles and challenges. In 2019, *Politico* published "Glass Ceiling" in which 11 women journalists, leaders and scholars weighed in on the major issues we face here in the US and globally. These included the lack of women in positions of power, the legacy of patriarchy, sexism, racism and economic inequality, trauma-centered feminism, normalizing misogyny, lack of respect for caregiving, and the current social political climate that seems to be a backlash to women's rights, especially reproductive rights. This book focuses on *internal* obstacles to women's transformation, while acknowledging the overarching socio-cultural climate. I believe that when women become empowered in overcoming their individual internal obstacles, we can create a critical tidal wave of external cultural social change over time.

The second major reason transformational change is different and more challenging for women is that we are socialized (and some evidence suggests biologically hard-wired) to be "other-centered." We are constantly having to calculate and balance our needs for growth and transition *within* the complex web of our intimate relationships, family member's demands and unequal, unbalanced social systems. The kind of transformation and change I write about here requires a self-centered perspective. It requires inward reflection, *self-*reflection. It demands courage, boldness, the willingness to say "NO" or "I've had ENOUGH", and set firm limits and boundaries. When a man makes major life changes and decisions, he is a visionary, "bold" and courageous. When similar visions or life changes are made by a woman, she is "selfish" at best, but she is more likely described as: a whore, a slut, a bitch, a ball-buster, a deceitful liar, or pick any derogatory word used by those threatened by women in power and self-sufficiency. I take it as a good omen that I have been called *all* of these names throughout my life's journey.

These are not just the musings of a feminist psychologist/ scholar. In fact, I often hesitate to use the term "feminist" as it is often used pejoratively in the mainstream media by those without understanding. I am *not* a man-hater. I have loved, and continue to love, many men and boys in my life as friends, colleagues, lovers, sons, family members, clients and students. The world we are currently living in is as damaging to men and boys as it is to girls and women.

I believe that we all have a masculine and feminine energy and that, in order to be spiritually and psychologically healthy, we need *both* of these aspects in balance. I remember one of my teachers/mentors, Anishinaabe elder Nick Hockings explaining that, in his traditional culture, boys were raised by their mothers, aunties and grandmothers until the age of seven or eight. During those formative years, they learned the feminine aspects of themselves: their intuition, emotionality and introspection. As they reached adolescence, they spent most of their time with their fathers, uncles and grandfathers to learn the more masculine aspects of their being. He believed that this created greater wholeness and balance as these boys reached manhood. The genocide and forced assimilation brought on by colonization of indigenous peoples destroyed traditions such as these that kept cultures in balance for eons, resulting in a plague of alcoholism and family violence.

For far too long, cultures that have devalued and denigrated the feminine have dominated most of the world. This overemphasis on masculine energies has caused great suffering for every living thing and has also resulted in the ecological crisis we now face. Nature has always been associated with the feminine; the themes in history, religion and mythology are cyclical and highly repetitive. There is an abundance of evidence that cultures with more balanced (Goddess-centered) cosmologies and social systems were far more peaceful and egalitarian than those representing the major dominating cultures of today. When we teach our children world history, it is literally from one war to another war. This creates the false perception that war is just human nature and we accept it. We never learn that there have been societies with hundred of years of peace.[1] Even among academics, peaceful societies are given little research and attention.

The ideas in this book are based on my own *lived*-experience, as well as the many women I have counseled over the last two decades. These ideas and themes are also found in poetry, mythology and literature from all over the world.

1. Robinson, A. (2016). The real utopia: This ancient civilization thrived without war. *New Scientist.* *https://www. newscientist. com/article/mg23130910-200-the-real-utopia-this-ancient-civilisation-thrived-without-war/(14 September 2016).*

Coleman, P. T., Fisher, J., Fry, D. P., Liebovitch, L. S., Chen-Carrel, A., & Souillac, G. (2021). How to live in peace? Mapping the science of sustaining peace: A progress report. *American Psychologist, 76*(7), 1113.

When I was in my early twenties, I remember reading, "A life that is worth living is worth recording." I started seriously journaling in 1988 and have continued this practice since. Having documented so many of my life-experiences, I can see patterns, trends and growth; I can see the ways I got trapped and stuck and ignored my instincts and intuition, and where I broke free. In the pages I see the pressure of the pen and use of *fuck* and its derivatives when I am in a rageful, negative psychological space. I see pages and pages of gratitude when I realized I have been so loved and supported spiritually and by so many people in my life. In my darkest times, it has given me great peace and comfort to re-read old passages and remember how I navigated previous dark waters. It is a means of learning and self-reflection for me that has been invaluable in my life. Many of the stories and things I share here I remember well or have developed a teaching narrative around *because* I felt it important to record and or document.

One of my teachers, Angelis Arrien, used say that our ancestors stand behind us and ask, "Is this the one who has come to break the harmful family patterns?" In my own life's journey and my years of work with clients, I am convinced that when we do our own healing work, we *are* healing the patterns from past generations and also impacting the generations that come after us. Science is now confirming that trauma is stored and passed on generationally in our DNA. I am conscious that as I do my own healing work, I am breaking the patterns and "mother-wounds" for my mother and grandmother as well.

In 2016, when my mother died in her eighties, I composed and read her eulogy. She was a woman who tried throughout her life to defy many of the social scripts and conventions with which she was raised. *She wanted to be a chatelaine.* She was not a great cook or housekeeper, but she could wield a mean hammer. She could fix all kinds of things and loved to build and sew. She was also a deeply-wounded woman. She described her own mother Pauline, as a "typical stage mother" who put her into dancing, modeling and acting starting at age three. My grandmother was herself wounded and not a nurturing woman but she was creative and resourceful enough to do what she needed to do to survive as woman in the 1930s and 40s. My mother went to Hollywood High School and was a part of the world of entertainment and movies. She was keenly aware of that world as full of predators and exploitation of child performers. When her father died at age 16, she was left even more vulnerable. She was wounded by having a pregnancy outside of wedlock with a man more than 20 years her senior and having her baby forcefully taken from her and given up for adoption. She was wounded throughout two marriages to abusive, emotionally shut-off, unhealthy men. She was widowed at age 58 and remained single until she died. When my sisters and I encouraged her to date and find a man, her response was always, "What do I want a man for? All they want is someone to clean and cook and do their laundry. I come and go and do what I please; I don't want anyone telling me what to do." Well, how could we argue with that? When I asked whether she missed or wanted sex, she looked at me like I had gone completely insane. "Why on earth would I want *that?*"

Typical of many women from her generation, sex was a wifely obligation to be endured and the way she was able to bring her much-wanted children into the world. When I was young woman exploring my sexuality, I asked her if my father was circumcised, and she looked at me wide-eyed and said, "How should I know?". You get the picture. She was, at that time, what some might call a man-hater but that's not exactly accurate. I would say she was, in her mind, *actively resisting the notion of male superiority.* She never missed an opportunity to point out the sheer stupidity, immaturity and ridiculousness of the men in our lives. My choices of boys and men typically guaranteed fresh grist for her man-mill. The only man she loved and respected was my sister's husband who she affectionately called "the Boss."

In reflecting on that period of my own life, I realize now that if I had found a man who I could truly deeply love and respect, it would have been a betrayal of this powerful aspect of our mother-daughter bond. We negatively bonded over having escaped terrible predatory relationships from our pasts and our present contempt of the human male species. In our wounded reactivity, we made a mother-daughter sport of proving to each other and whoever was paying attention that we were every bit as smart and capable as men at doing just about everything. When I told her I was marrying for the second time, she told me quite bluntly that I was "making the biggest mistake of my life." I do not think that was entirely true because I had, by that time, tallied up quite a magnificent collection of big mistakes. She was right in *some* ways about many things that she foresaw in that relationship. She had a different vision for me and and my life and clearly saw some dangers and potential traps, but that part of the story comes later.

In the last several years of my mom's life, she started what I would call a 'life-in-review.' She had me search the internet for months to try and find a man who in the 1940s took her on a date "held her hand sweetly" and "took her to an opera" something she was romanticizing as the most powerful "love" experience of her life. She was regretting that she never found or experienced "real love" which is so sad given that she had been married twice and had five children. Having pretty good online sleuthing skills and his name and approximate age, I believe I found him, or his obituary anyway. But she refused to believe that it was *her* love. She always kept hope and kept me searching.

After I realized the fruitlessness of finding a love from decades ago, my gift to her instead was purchasing opera season tickets. In the last few years of my mom's life, I took the time and space to make wonderful memories of matinees and long lunches in the bistro at the Civic Opera House in Chicago. At one such lunch, after a bottle of red wine, she confided, "I

always worried the most about you. You are the most like me."
Truthfully, I was stunned and speechless. I thought I couldn't
be *more* different than her. It is only now, years later, that I
understand the deeper meaning of what she said. Despite
my "feminist" spirit, living as a strong, successful, highly-
educated woman, she saw my cages and self-imprisonment.
Despite all of my success, worldly achievements and family
life, she still held firmly that I was trapped in the wrong
partnership and hence a life that kept me working so hard at
survival that there was little time for joy, creativity or literally
anything that mattered. She sensed on a deep-knowing level
my unhappiness, restlessness and depression. In her last few
years, she watched me break free and transform to become
the chatelaine in my own life. I think it gave her great relief,
satisfaction and peace. She never stopped believing in a "one
true love" and she held that hope for both of us until the day
she died.

In her eulogy, I spoke about our favorite opera: *The Barber
of Seville* by Rossini. Unlike many other operas where female
characters are deceived, betrayed and meet tragic fates, Rosina
is a heroine who outsmarts the scheming men in the story and
ultimately wins her freedom and her true love. In my *mother's*
interpretation of the story, I believe that she thought both of
us were 'Rosinas.' I have not been able to set foot in the opera
house since she died. Though I am independent and free,
only time will tell if I am truly a Rosina. What I *do* know for
certain is that ***I am a chatelaine.***

I believe that healing and transformation travel through time and up and down our family bloodlines. I believe that they travel not only to benefit future generations (our descendants) but that they also can have a profound effect on our ancestors and our family lines. I come from a highly diverse and colorful family history of both victimhood and leadership, of healing and tragedy. I do believe that my ancestors are standing behind me, hoping I will have the stamina and courage to break many harmful family and cultural patterns. I am a healer and leader of women. I am dedicated to this work, if for nothing else, then for my grandmothers, aunts, sisters, my mother Betty Jo and my daughter Ciara.

Me and my mother with my daughter Ciara (2009)

Introduction

Chatelaine is an old French word that has two meanings, It originally referred to the lady of a manor, chateau or castle. She had all the keys to all of the rooms the resources and wealth and, as such, she needed *many* keys. She wore these on a ring or belt around her waist. The word eventually referred to a belt or pin of keys and household or sewing implements that a  lady would wear around her waist or pinned to her clothing. During the Victorian era these were very popular and were customized according to a lady's stature or profession. Some nurses wore special chatelaines with tools. I've heard these described as a 'hanging Swiss army knife.'

I don't recall the first time I heard this term. But I do clearly remember when I owned the energy of this persona. During a

particularly painful and stressful period of my life when I was trying to leave behind a very unhappy marriage, a mentor and healer who I was working with had repeatedly pointed out to me that I was over-resourced for every challenge I was facing. When I would describe my marriage situation, he referred to it as a "cage." He insisted that I come to terms with the fact that I already held the 'keys' to my own freedom. I just could not see it. He would say to me, "How can someone with such *vision* not have clear vision for their own life and future?" He was exasperated with me many times when I recounted all the endless reasons I could not break free: finances didn't allow it , the timing was bad, my children would suffer, what would happen to my dogs?, my horses?, my elderly mother's health was declining, I was in the midst of the tenure process at the university, I had a grueling schedule ... on and on. I was walking across an overgrown marsh with my two dogs and I felt somehow I had stepped back in time. In this brief, numinous moment, I had the thought: *I am a chatelaine.* It was almost as though I could feel the keys jingling at my waist.

I have experiences like this all the time. In Jungian psychology this is called a 'numinous' experience. The major milestones or moments that punctuate my transitions--I can name them all like keys or tools on my chatelaine belt. When I listen carefully to the stories of other women, I find that they have these moments too. They have the numinous moments, the dreams, the "wake-up calls", the health scares, the prayers of desperation in the middle of the night. Why is it, then, that change for us is so difficult?

Not only am I a cross-culturally trained psychologist and healer, my personal and professional practice is grounded in depth psychology. This means that I use symbols, dreams, images, intuition and synchronicity (meaningful coincidences) and focus on understanding the dynamics of the unconscious as a means to release suffering and ultimately attain freedom or what we call the *liberation of being*. Healing is associated with allowing what has been repressed, rejected, denied or ignored to come forward so that we can understand its significance, integrate it and allow it to transform our consciousness. In addition to our own psyches, I also attend to the ways in which unconscious processes express themselves in our society and culture and how this affects our own psyche. Depth psychology in its very nature is cross-cultural and interdisciplinary. Those of us who use this approach use synchronicities, signs and symbols to guide us on our healing paths.

For the last several thousand years women in most cultures on the planet have been socialized, well-trained and imprinted within our families and communities to live in 'cages.' Women have been *domesticated*. Doesn't it seem telling that when referring to animals and women we use the same terminology? Animal "husbandry", for example? Domestication involves the control over the life and especially *reproduction* of one species by another species for the means of securing resources. The domestication of women has been the major task of organized religions since the spread of the Hebrew Old Testament myth of Adam and Eve and the violent overthrow of Goddess-based cosmologies in favor of those with a single male God.

Women have forgotten and repressed our most basic wild instincts. So much so, that we don't know how to *pay attention* and recognize traps and cages. It might look good and smell good but we often fail to see the steel jaws so that we can walk on or run away. We don't know how to teach our young daughters how to sniff out a predator, trust her body wisdom and most basic instincts to avoid traps and cages. One of my favorite works that has shaped much of my thinking is Dr. Clarissa Pinkola Estés' *Women Who Run With the Wolves*. She uses storytelling to illustrate many themes of women and their true natures. She makes the most salient point that if girls and women do not make a place for their true "wildish" nature, that nature manifests itself in self-destructive ways.

I am a life-long horsewoman, and women are a lot like horses. In fact, there are many ancient myths (such as the Celtic Epona) depicting horses as the embodiment of the divine feminine. Despite being domesticated for over 6,000 years, horses have their instincts and wild-natures still readily accessible. Horses will 'activate' their true natures when they are afraid and faced with a threat. We can access our deeply-hidden wild natures and heal ourselves from where we are instinct-injured. We *can* learn how to escape traps and cages and also learn not to return to them. Those of us with scars from our experiences in traps and cages can teach and support other girls and women by sharing our stories and the things we've learned. In the process of writing and sharing my stories with the women I've worked with, I became aware that I had a *process* or a *system* for how I navigated change and freed myself from situations and negative patterns in order to life a life of liberation, joy and vision. The system can be described as:

1) Start with a vision of a symbol that you can use as a "North Star"

2) Use the power of *writing* (journaling) honestly, clearly and consistently

3) Recognize cages and traps

4) Gather energy and reclaim power

5) Clear the hearth

6) Re-spark the flames of passion and vision

7) Imagine a more detailed vision

8) Commit to daily, inspired action toward your vision

9) Continue to repeat the process as your life transforms and evolves. (The work is never done but becomes more joyful and fulling each time).

This work is comprised of sections. First, we'll start with a vision (sense) of desire, even if it is very vague. I give a mediation for you to ask your soul-mind for a symbol to hold and revisit during the transformation process. Next, I identify the cages or traps we need to get out of to execute our desires and vision. I explore common traps and cages--the different ways that women become trapped in lives and situations that may be unfulfilling, harmful, or worse, soul-killing. These include harmful relationships, self-betrayal and self-abandonment, instinct injury and overwork and exhaustion. The keys for liberation are tools that we can develop, use and keep. The keys are core principles such as intuition, intention, body wisdom, mentors and connection to nature that enable women to gather the resources and healing energy to free themselves from traps and cages and begin to rediscover their creativity, passion and heart-centered lives. The final section is on getting more detailed on our vision and living as the chatelaine of our own lives. Being a chatelaine means creating and committing to a life of joy and passion that aligns with our life's dreams.

Before we get started on our liberation journey, it is highly recommended that you read the next session on "How to Use This Book."

Here is to the chatelaine that lives in us all.

♟ ♟ ♟

How to Use This Book:
Accessing Your Magic Powers

There is no magic.
Life is full of magic.

When I was a young girl, my favorite TV shows were Bewitched and I Dream of Jeannie. I was convinced that I too was magic. I was magic and I am magic. Miracles and magic happen to me everyday, people and things show up at just the right times. I am protected and guided throughout my days. I do pretty, beautiful magic all the time. It is only by looking backward I can see that the really big magic was very, very messy and sometimes ugly. The big transformations took tremendous courage, persistence and above all, faith and vision. I access my magic powers through the power of words/writing, stillness/solitude and bold, focused action.

The Power of Words: Writing

Throughout my life's journey I have found journaling *by hand* with pen and paper, specifically--the act of ***writing,*** to be a key element in change, transition and creating my life's vision. My therapy clients quickly learn that they need to bring a notebook or paper for their work with me. I find myself frequently saying, "write this down." I encourage *all* of the adult clients I work with to journal, to write as much as possible as a key element in the process of healing, transformation and change. There is power in the written word that should not be underestimated. Spiritually, the act of handwriting one's mental and emotional processes, internal dialogue and perspectives on external events, helps us access a doorway to recognize patterns and systems that trap us as well as the keys to set ourselves free. It utilizes a different area of our brains than just mulling things over in our minds. Since a high percentage of thought is repetitive, the act of writing allows us to see patterns more readily as well as tracking our progress through time. Creating a journaling habit helps us to get clarity, prioritize goals, dreams, problems and fears. Journaling allows us to track relationship patterns in black and white so we can decide which to keep and which to leave. Journaling is a way of creating and documenting an intimate conversation with our own minds. At the end of each chapter, there are a series of journal prompts/questions to get the processes started, as it relates to both the cages and the keys for liberation and vision. It is important not to ignore or skip this step. I explain below not only *why* journaling is powerful but also the obstacles people often face with trying to develop this practice.

Diaries versus Journals:

First, the way I am defining a journal is beyond what we typically think of as a diary. A diary is a chronological recording of events and in and of itself, is not sufficient to bring about change. A journal, on the other hand, is a written conversation that we have with ourselves, with spirit and sometimes imagined conversations with others in writing. It can also include dreams that we want to remember upon awakening. Jungians record dreams as a means to bridge unconscious messages with our conscious minds so that we can receive the messages encoded in them. It is a conversation we have with ourselves that not only helps us get to know our own minds and processes intimately, it provides a space for the evolution of our thinking, the opportunity for critical self-reflection, awareness of our contradictions and negative patterns or beliefs that no longer serve us. It becomes a way to focus our minds on our visions and intentions and to track and chronicle our growth and change process.

I *do* recommend writing by hand rather than typing notes in a computer or a phone for a number of reasons. Unlike typing on a keyboard, writing by hand engages a number of brain functions all at once. Handwriting requires hand-eye coordination, language, memory, creativity, insight, logic, spacial intelligence and abstract thought. When writing with pen and paper, a collection of cells in the Reticular Activating System (RAS) at the base of our brains is engaged. The RAS is the filtering system for the information your brain needs to process. I tell clients it filters out the garbage and clutter in our minds and helps us get to the heart of things much more quickly. It *forces us* to get clear. It directs the brain to pay close attention to what you are focusing on in writing. In other words, the act of writing brings information to the forefront of our brains and focuses our attention. Writing consistently as a spiritual and psychological practice allows us to bridge and make meaning from our internal and external processes. There are decades of research that provide evidence that journaling can be an important component to mental health. In the 1960s and 70s, depth psychologist Ira Progoff, created a system called the Intensive Journal Method that used and described journal writing as having the ability to draw each person's life towards wholeness. His methods have used journaling for both clinical issues such as depression as well as issues like enhancing creativity and overcoming writer's block. I use custom journaling processes or prompts for each client based on the issues they are working on.

Despite my imploring them to do so, a number of clients and students have difficulty with journaling. The most common blocks or obstacles are fears about privacy, time and space, and judgement or censorship.

When women do not feel that they have the respect for privacy in their own homes to freely journal without fear this is a HUGE red flag in and of itself. Journaling of this type is the most intimate conversation with self and a window into our very souls. It is natural to feel afraid, especially because we have often experienced traumas or boundary violations on our life's path. In writing this section, I was reminded that both of my ex-husbands not only spied on me by reading my journals - they were adamant that our relationships would be so much better if I wasn't writing in "my book." It is only through wisdom and reflection of this vantage point that I realize they were aware that this writing process was a powerful practice and one that intimately led to my freedom from both of these relationships. Fear for one's privacy is an indication of relationship boundary issues that are much more serious than just the journaling. To really know one's mind and soul intimately there must be space for introspection, integration and inner-dialogue. If the fear of others not respecting your journal process is the case, I suggest strategies for journaling (and keeping the journal) in places that don't call attention to the process or leave it open for discovery. Women I work with who have this concern often journal on their lunch hour at work and keep their journals locked there. The other issue of confidentiality is one I also am conscious of in that journals are our raw, naked most private thoughts. Dedicating someone highly trustworthy to steward and destroy our journals if something should happen to us (like when we die) can provide a greater sense of comfort with writing in the most truthful uncensored way.

Journaling effectively takes time and space to develop. I have found that establishing a routine or ritual time and place for journal work is very helpful. The time should be when you are not too tired (I like to journal to start my day) and where you can sit undisturbed for at least 10-20 minutes in the beginning. I love to journal on vacation because the time and space are more plentiful and some of my best insights, ideas and plans come when I am relaxed and away from my daily schedule. It does not need to be a long session, journal until the process feels complete. There will be an ebb and flow to journaling - with times of great change, stress or transition requiring more journal time and energy than times that are relatively more calm and settled.

The last obstacle to address here is judgment and the self-critic. The self-critic is that annoying awful roommate in our head (who we should have evicted a long time ago). The practice and discipline of journaling of this type requires us to manage and suspend our judgment and tendency to correct or censor our writing. Writing is a push-pull process between the frontal lobes and the temporal lobes of the brain. When we have what is called "writer's block" it is because the judgment (frontal lobe processes) have taken over and we no longer have the push-pull dynamic of the temporal lobe activity, thus writing comes to a screeching halt. I have found remedies for this include writing with our non-dominant hand or writing very quickly as to not give attention to the censoring process and allow the words and subconscious to flow freely. Learn to write and record all impressions and impulses--*everything counts;* do not censor. This is especially important because we are often in the habit of ignoring, denying or blocking-out a

Some of my journals from *years* of this process

Journaling Process

1. Dedicate a notebook, a good time (10 minutes, to start) and a quiet private place to journal.

2. Start with dating your journal. Anchor the time and place and "recap" of what is going on in your life at this moment in time

3. Practice with the prompts, free-write or create your own intention for the journal session

4. Journal as freely as you can without censoring or editing until you feel like your heart is complete

5. Keep your journal and the ritual of writing sacred; it is "soul" writing

6. Do it again and again and again

The Power of Words: Speech

In the world of myth, magic and fairytales, all characters understand the tremendous power of words. Words can be incantations or curses that have *real* physical consequences. Spiritual traditions since the beginning of time have taught us about the power of words in the physical world and in creation. Words have their own energy and quality and this *does* affect us and the world around us. Modern physics and science is confirming what mystics have known all along. *Words matter.* The effects that words have on developing children as early as in the womb are well-documented. However, people disconnected from our connection with the natural world may miss that words also impact the natural environment around us. For example, words have been found to affect water crystals. Japanese researcher and healer, Dr. Masaru Emoto, conducted experiments on water molecules. These experiments showed human thoughts and intentions can physically alter the molecular structure of water. In another study on the effects of words on plants, results showed that positivity in the environment and words had a significant positive effect on plant growth. Plant seeds under the influence of the positive words had a higher germination rate, and these plants grew taller, larger, and healthier than those in negative environments.

The indigenous elders I've worked with over my lifetime did not use curse words. They too understood the energy and power behind words. In various stages of my life, I have cursed like a sailor. Sometimes I found that a few 'fucks' were the only way I could express the intensity of my emotions. However, as I've tried to be more self-conscious and aware of the energy associated with words - I find myself using curse words less and less. Additionally, observing how I speak about my life, my dreams and others has had a very positive impact on the quality and energy in my life.

The most important words are the words to say to yourself. The self-critic, that terrible annoying roommate in your mind, is a voice that you need to come to terms with and have mastery over. It especially has no place in the healing room. I bring this up throughout the book. Speaking in the most positive, compassionate and self-affirming way has the power to transform how you feel and respond to every situation you encounter.

Words Awareness Practice

1. Start tracking and paying closer attention to your words and phrases

2. Do the things you talk about and share with others support you and the life you want to be living ?

3. Track self-talk. Pay close attention to the themes and messages that you are telling yourself everyday and note those that need to shift.

Stillness and Solitude

Modernist English author Virginia Woolf published *A Room of One's Own* in 1929. In it she explored how the creative genius of women has been lost to the world due to gender inequality and social conditions and beliefs about women and their capabilities for creative generatively. She recognized the need for time and space for reflection and accessing our inner-world. I wonder what essay she would pen now, almost one hundred years later? Would she applaud the strides we have made? Would she see the many ways that we still do not have a 'room' of our own? I suspect that she would, in her acute powers of observation and perception, see all the ways in which women are still thwarted from achieving their artistic and creative genius. We may have gained greater financial freedom and equality but at a very steep price. Feminist writers have been writing for sometime now about the phenomena called the 'second shift', where women in the workforce return to home for a second shift of running the household and childcare responsibilities.

As I write this section in year two of the global pandemic, research from Lean In, the women's organization founded by Facebook COO Sheryl Sandberg, examines how women working from home are faring during the Covid-19 pandemic compared with men. Their findings, at least to many women in that situation, are likely unsurprising: Women with full-time jobs, a partner, and children report spending a combined

71 hours a week on child care, elder care, and household chores -- compared with 51 hours for men. A quarter of women are experiencing physical symptoms of severe anxiety, compared with just 11 percent of men. Women of color are facing an even more challenging situation: 75 percent of black and Latina women spend a combined 21-plus hours per week on housework, compared with just over half of white women; they also spend more time on child care and elder care than their white counterparts.

What this means for accessing inner-wisdom and creativity is that we simply do not have enough time, energy and space in our lives. Since our mind has superpowers, or magic powers as I like to say, having time and space for stillness is essential.

Research indicates that 20 minutes of meditation is the equivalent of 4-5 hours of sleep[2]. Many women I work with have great difficulty finding five minutes to themselves, let alone 20 minutes, and this is problematic. Like any change, starting with a few minutes and being successful with making that a habit and then adding a bit more time is a strategy that works. Women need to carve out that time in their days often in creative ways. But stillness is important for balance, for recharging our energy, for accessing the soul-mind (our inner wisdom) and our creativity. *A relaxed mind is a creative mind.*

---

2. Treven, S., & Potocan, V. (2005). Training programmes for stress management in small businesses. *Education+ Training.*

As you begin the process of change and transformation, stillness and the ability to quiet your mind will be even more important. There are literally hundreds of ways to quiet the mind and mediate - including many that are using apps and technology. Ancient physical practices such as yoga and tai chi are designed to prepare the body for stillness--so we can access the deeper levels of mind.

Stillness Practice Dedication

Think of stillness of the mind and body (such as meditation) as a way of 'recharging your battery' and also tapping into your power.

1) How much time do you sit in stillness or mediation right now? If this is difficult, start with five minutes of quiet and work up to 20 minutes over time.

2) If formal meditation does not suit you at this time, or seems to difficult, try making a mental list all the things you are grateful for, or simply setting an intention for your day.

3) Try various forms of meditation. There are many to chose from.

On Solitude: The Need for Space

I write about this here in the start of the book because I know that any transformation process will require energy and focused thought to complete. It is during periods of solitude that we get to know ourselves intimately, healing our wounds and patterns, as well as setting intentions for the life that we want to create. If a woman has intense fears around being alone, it indicates that she is in need of professional spiritual or psychological support.

I have learned over the years that I have a high need for space and solitude. I used to think that if I was with the right *person* or partner that I could learn and adjust my needs for less space. This does not mean that I don't like the company of others, or being in close relationships and having adventures, it is just that in order to feel at my best and most balanced, I need regular alone time. As one woman I work with says, "My three best friends are me, myself and I."

It has taken me years to learn that not only is is not true for me, but that many women have difficulties with creating time and space for solitude in their lives. This is a highly individual need of course, but I am addressing it here because I find that our culture does not honor and understand the need for solitude. Historically, if a woman was 'idle' with too much solitude, it was feared she would be tempted or coopted by the devil. There is a reason that the witches in fairy tales all lived alone in the woods! Very often in Western culture we use time outs (forced alone time) as punishment and the term *loner* is negative. I prefer the term *contemplative*. It is much more fancy- I am a contemplative chatelaine.

The ability to be alone is an important dimension of self-growth. When we spend time alone we face our emotions and our wounds. To get comfortable with being alone, we need to be willing to embrace our feelings, weaknesses and strengths. During periods of alone time we can hear the voice of our intuition and access our superpower of focused thought.

Recent psychological research also indicates that there are many benefits to chosen alone time and that this is needed whether a person is an extrovert or introvert.[3] In a recent survey on rest and well-being (the largest to date) 18,000 people from 134 countries made time to take part in what was quite a lengthy survey devised by Hubbub--an international group of academics, artists, poets, and mental health experts--showing what a pressing issue rest is in the modern world. The results of the survey indicated that *all* of the restful activities were things people did alone. Reading was the top activity followed by spending time in nature, listening to music, and doing nothing in particular. Some researchers and psychologists are rethinking the emphasis on our needs for closeness and socialization and finding that balance with chosen alone time has a number of benefits that *improved* relationships with others.

---

3. For examples see:
https://www.nytimes.com/2019/10/28/smarter-living/the-benefits-of-being-alone.html

Leavitt, C. E., Butzer, B., Clarke, R. W., & Dvorakova, K. (2021). Intentional solitude and mindfulness: The benefits of being alone. *The Handbook of Solitude: Psychological Perspectives on Social Isolation, Social Withdrawal, and Being Alone*, 340-350.

So even with individual variations on the need for space and alone time, I find that the majority of women I work with get very little alone time and space. They don't know how to ask for this without guilt and sometimes their loved ones take the need for alone time personally. When I talk with women about their fantasies, not surprisingly they often involve "disappearing" and traveling somewhere alone. Somewhere where no one knows them or wants anything from them. I understand my mother not wanting to get married again after she was widowed at 58. It was socially acceptable for the first time in her life to live alone and, while she was fit and healthy for another 20 years, it seemed she was very happy. She rejected ever wanting to be with a partner again because she said it would be too constraining on her time, energy and desires.

Asking for alone time and space requires delicate communication and conversation skills and a willingness to set some boundaries around our time and energy. We need to let our loved ones know that this is necessary for us to bring balance to our lives and to make sure we are bringing our best selves into our relationships. As I looked at and tracked through journaling my own patterns of how I would create alone time and space, I also started seeing this pattern in other women. When not getting enough alone time and space, I tend to get irritable and find the presence of another person to be a form of pressure. Because I didn't fully own or understand how to ask for space without hurting another's feelings or feeling a sense of guilt or self-indulgence, on a unconscious level, I discovered that in the past I used four strategies to create solitude: 1) sickness or injury 2) conflict 3) overwork 4) work-related travel. I write this here so that you can see if any of these needs or strategies resonate with you and *if* they do you can become more conscious of asking for what you need rather than using harmful unconscious means.

1) Sickness and injury: The major health crises in my life have all preceded big transformation. It has often took being flat on my back staring up at the ceiling to hear the whispers of my spirit and soul-mind calling for change. I've made a conscious commitment to listen and take (demand if needed) time and space so that my body doesn't need to get sick or injured for me to have this need met.

2) Conflict: I noticed that not only would I be irritated by the presence of others when I needed alone time and space (they weren't really *doing* anything just *being in my space* asking or doing their normal stuff) I would pick a fight and create an explosion so that we would storm off to our separate places and I could then be alone. The harm of this strategy is obvious. I have committed to being self- aware of this pattern and to seek what I need before I get grumpy.

3) Overwork: I used to hide out in my work and in my office. The problem with this is that it creates a pattern of overworking and doesn't meet the need for solitude and recharging. Many women I work with use work in

place of true rejuvenating solitude because it is socially and culturally acceptable and we can justify it to our loved ones. I have committed to telling the truth to myself and others about what I need so I don't use the pattern of overwork as a means for taking space.

4) Work-related travel: I used to travel a lot for work and during my Ph.D. program. While this was necessary, I also discovered that I *love* to travel alone. I also enjoy traveling with my loved ones but I also find that, before and after, I need alone time to rebalance myself. Because travel for work was something that justified my need for solitude, I have often taken on travel-related work that I didn't need to do - just to have that time and space. This additional travel-time often has sidetracked me from goals and other projects that I could have put time and energy into - if I knew how to ask for space.

The Need for Alone Time and Space Exercise

1) Do you have alone time and space? How do you spend it?

2) What resistance or fears come up when you are facing time and space alone?

3) Think about possible unconscious patterns around time and space - are there any negative things you do to create alone time?

4) If you had complete freedom to chose how you would spend a day, what would you do?

Bold, Focused Action:
Pray an Earnest Prayer--and Move Your Feet

At 29 years old, I was confused and exhausted. I traveled alone to Mexico to recharge and rethink my life. I sat cross-legged on the beach in Xtapa facing the Pacific at night as the full moon shone high in the night sky. In a self-created ritual, I prayed to the grandmother ocean, the moon and the sky with a tea-light candle at my feet.

"I will do whatever it takes...," I whispered out loud but with intensity and urgency. "I will do what my soul came here to do."

Then, at that precise moment, a wave that was arriving with the rising tide – outside of my awareness crashed over me and took into the sea my flip-flops, the tea-light and my hotel key. That wave was a small foreshadowing of big changes to come. My prayer set into motion a complete dismantling of the life I had - so that I could build anew. Looking back on this- now being much older and wiser, I would have asked for a more gentle unfolding of doing what my soul came here to do. Now I always follow requests adding "with grace and ease"

The final recommendation for using this book is to know that during your transformation process, there will be times for bold, focused action. One of the issues I have with self-help books (or even therapy for that matter) is that we can cycle or get caught in a loop, and become frozen or trapped because we are afraid to take action towards the change and the life we are trying to create. There have been times I have told clients to come back when they have decided on one committed action.

When I say "pray and move your feet", I mean "take the time to get mentally and spiritually focused and get into alignment with your soul-mind, *then* take action." Use stillness and solitude to access your intuition and wisdom and then trust that guidance and move your feet.

Along your journey there will be a few leaps of faith and committed actions that you must take. In many myths and stories using big magic (as opposed to pretty little magic) means destroying an ordinary life or existence to dive deep headfirst into extraordinary existence. This takes wisdom, focused intent, tremendous courage and patience. Only the strongest women will dare to use this big magic power but the rewards are phenomenal. As you read these words, know you are loved, observed and supported in your journey. So let's begin.

Start With Your VISION for Your Life
What is the transformation you desire?

At a particularly low point in my life in my late 40s, I was mentally, physically and spiritually worn out. I sought to work with a traditional healer to 'revision' my life. In a state of deep meditation and relaxation, they asked me to call up a vision or a symbol for my soul's-work to guide me towards the major life changes I was about to undertake. I kept seeing a white horse. I found a statue of a white horse and placed it where I would see it everyday to remind me of the larger vision and journey of my life, even when I had no idea what the details were going to be or how I was going to get there. Now I have the understanding of Epona, and the relationship of this to the Divine Feminine, the expression of which is my soul's mission in this lifetime.

Throughout human history, Polaris, or the North Star, has been an easily seen, bright constellation almost in alignment with the North Pole that serves as a navigational guide. Metaphorically speaking, we *all* need a reference point or navigational "North Star." This is the first and most critical step in the journey of transformation. You *have* to have a sense of what you desire as a part of your transformation process. For example, do you need greater balance in your life? To live with more ease and grace? To have more joy? To experience freedom? To have a deeper spiritual sense of yourself and your life? Do you have unfulfilled life dreams or goals? When you were drawn to this book, the deepest part of our wisdom-self, or *soul-mind* as I like to call it, was longing for change and transformation. Often we know this intuitively but we get discouraged because the details are vague and sketchy. Often we've spent so much of our lives pleasing and meeting the needs of others that we've never taken the time to get in touch with what *we* desire.

You were meant to live an extraordinary life. You can transcend the ordinary or unfulfilling life you may be living right now. This takes bravery, honesty patience and a willingness to risk and let go of things and people that do not serve you.

Getting in touch with our yearnings and desires helps us to have the energy to remove obstacles and get out of our traps and 'cages.' It is perfectly okay if your vision is unclear at the present time; don't let that stop you. Focus on the qualities you want to experience and embrace in your life. You can create a symbol to guide you, to remind you and energize you when you need it. You will revisit it and get clearer and more detailed as you go through the transformation process. Sometimes we are just too exhausted to create a detailed vision and there is much releasing, rebalancing and strengthening that needs to happen to get clear. However you can always ask for a symbol to come to your mind/imagination to be your North Star on the journey. If you already have a clear vision or goals in mind, this exercise can further strengthen your commitment and provide you with a potent symbol when you need inspiration or energy.

This exercise is a guided imagery meditation. My suggestion is that you read it aloud in your own voice and record it to play it back. You can also access a recording of this on my website at *www.Drarieahnmb.com*

To prepare for this exercise, find a quite place where you will not be disturbed for at least 20 minutes. Have a journal and pen handy to take notes (or draw) and find a comfortable place to sit or lie down where you will not have to think about your body. (If your body is uncomfortable, you will find it very difficult to quiet and focus your mind).

Visioning Transformation:
Find Your North Star Symbol

Put your body in a place where you are comfortable and don't have to think about it. You can lie down on your back or sit with your back resting and your feet flat to the floor. Close your eyes softly. Start with some slow rhythmic deep breaths. Don't work to take the breath in, just fill completely and exhale completely with ease.

Breathe in relaxation and breath out tension. Allow your body to progressively relax. Start with your face: relax your forehead and the tiny muscles around your eyes and let that relaxation spread like a wave all the way to the soles of your feet. Relax your jaw and loosen your tongue from the roof of your mouth.

Take another breath and, as you exhale, let your shoulders drop. Feel your upper arms relax, then your lower arms and then your hands. Extend your fingers out, breathe in and then, on the exhale, wiggle the fingers slightly and let go of any tension you were holding. Relax your back body and let it be supported. Relax your abdomen, then your upper legs, then lower legs; feel your feet. Wiggle the toes slightly and let go of any tension you are holding.

Allow yourself to feel totally relaxed and at ease. Whenever you relax like this you receive great benefit to your mind, body and spirit - and this is so.

You have a mind and your mind is important to you. It holds all of your memories, knowledge and experiences. You have a mind but you are so much more than that.

You have a body and your body is important to you. You can be still or in movement, hungry or full, tired or energized, tense or relaxed. Your body can change and be many things but you are so much more than just your physical body.

You have emotions and feelings. They can change in a moment; your feelings are important indicators to your level of alignment with who you truly are. They are important to you but you are much more than your emotions, your body or your mind... you are a point of consciousness--a soul. The true you has always existed before you were in this physical body having your experiences of this life... before you had these memories, knowledge and emotions you've gained while on your physical trail. Acknowledge and feel this ancient energy of the true you. Let your facial expression, breathing and posture reflect this blended energy of your personality/identity in this current lifetime with the true eternal you, your true higher self within you.

When you decided to come into this life, you had a goal or mission. There were things you wanted to accomplish and things you wanted to learn and contribute to the world. You can call this your higher purpose or your soul's purpose. In the process of becoming who you are right now, you may have forgotten these things or perhaps got a little side-tracked. That's okay you've learned much already and everything has prepared you in some way for your purpose even if it is not clear at this moment.

To align with this purpose even if the details are not clear at this time, you can ask your soul to send you a symbol to hold in your mind. You can draw this symbol or find something physical that reminds you of this symbol. You can use this as your North Star to keep you on track and help you navigate your path as the details become clearer and clearer. You can send light and energy to this symbol whenever you are discouraged or need inspiration and this is so.

Ask your soul now for a sign or symbol and see this like on a movie screen in your minds-eye now.

Give gratitude for this time, connection and symbol and when you are ready, flutter your eyes open and return to the room. Be sure to take any notes you want to remember in your journal.

Draw or hold the image of that symbol in your mind.

The
Cages

Introduction to Cages:

Eyes-Wide-Open
Seeing and Telling the Truth

The goal of this book is to illustrate a *system* for change and liberation. The first step *must* be an honest, eyes-wide-open assessment of where we are trapped or stuck in 'cages'. These may be cages we have willing walked in to, self-created unconsciously or they may be family or cultural legacies that we carry. Regardless, our first task is honesty and truth-telling on where and what types of cages we may be trapped in. I want to emphasize here that this is without judgment or shame. (God knows we've had enough of that energy for the last several thousand years!). Women can plan their escapes from cages whether these are destructive life patterns, mates/ lovers or jobs. We know how to stall for time, bide our time and plan our strategy. We call up and gather all of our power internally before we make an external change. Sometimes the suffering or pressure becomes too great and we explode into change. Either way, this book is both and understanding of strategies of using our power, instincts and intuition to plan our way out, or understand the explosions and prevent future entrapment so we can live with greater freedom, joy and vision.

There are a few ways to approach the cages section. First you can read chapter by chapter and journal your way through the cages and see what comes up, or you can see which cage draws your attention right now and then progress from there. Consciousness is the way out the of the trap - the way to freedom. Women must recognize and be willing to stand by what they see and know what needs to be done about it.

🔑🔑🔑

Relationship Cages:
Gather and Reclaim Your Power

I've always had a high pain tolerance, as did my mother. In that regard we were own own worst enemies. I was taught very early to endure pain and discomfort. I had journaled for years, trying to figure out (fix) my marriage. I cried rivers that doused my fires of rage and frustration. It took a major health crisis to finally make me face this cage. When I woke up from my left-breast lumpectomy, I felt a sense of apathy and indifference. I didn't really care whether I woke up or not. As I more fully regained consciousness, I realized how terrifying and serious it was to not care. I knew I would rather die than stay in my marriage.

Photo by Christopher Windus on Unsplash

One of the most challenging cages to recognize is what I am calling the *relationship cage*. What I mean by this is the ways in which women get trapped in relationships that are toxic, high-conflict or *soul-killing* or *life-force draining*. The first two, (toxic and high conflict) are fairly easy to recognize. The latter is much more difficult to identify because as females, we are heavily imprinted, reinforced and socialized to be "other-centered." In my practice, often women experience health scares as wake-up calls. Once a woman I was counseling briefly was praying everyday for guidance about whether to leave her toxic marriage. Being religious, she struggled with leaving her long-term marriage even though it was clearly harmful for her to stay and her partner was unwilling to consider therapy or change. Her prayers were 'answered' when she had a freak accident, breaking her left ring finger so she had to have her wedding ring cut off in the emergency room! Many women I have worked with suffer from mysterious chronic illnesses and pain, which in some cases, is the deepest wisdom of the body manifesting their pain and misery.

Women are often instinct-injured when we are very young girls. Early in our lives, we often develop a high pain tolerance depending on our early experiences in our families and culture of origin. If we are instinct-injured through abuse, betrayal, adults failing to nurture, failing to meet our emotional, physical or spiritual needs or failing to protect us, we may not recognize predatory persons or imbalanced unhealthy relationship dynamics. Our families, cultures or religious teachings can create beliefs that our role is to endure or to suffer. Women collectively, and individually need to recognize that this pattern and belief systems is thousands of years old. Beliefs are *not facts*. They are nothing more than ideas that we've thought so much collectively and individually, repetitively, that they *seem* to be truths or feel true.

While imbalanced or unhealthy marriages/intimate relationships can obviously be relationship cages, so can our relationships with significant others. Children (including our adult children), brothers and sisters, parents, in-laws, friends and co-workers can be cages in and of themselves. Recognizing these cages requires honest, eyes-wide-open truth-telling. Women need to take an honest inventory of where and how they are using their precious life-energy. Cages are created when we 1) take too much responsibility for another person, 2) are driven by the primal fears of abandonment or engulfment, 3) are unconscious of our family or origin patterns and amalgams, 4) don't take responsibility for being 'adult' in relationships and 5) don't know how to set limits and boundaries appropriately. Human relationships are our greatest joy and our greatest challenge . Most therapists or spiritual teachers would agree that our most difficult relationships can be our best teachers.

1. Taking too much responsibility for another person.

In taking an honest inventory of relationships, it is critical to assess the level of responsibility we are taking for the people we are closest to. It should be obvious that we are not talking about babies or small children here, or others for whom we *must* be caretakers because they *physically* can't care for themselves, but rather, our older children or the other adults in our lives who *are* capable but for whatever reason are *unwilling to* step into self-sufficiency. In its extreme form- it would be codependence (an issue that is often addressed in therapy). But the more subtle forms of this can be an insidious trap. If you find yourself working harder on behalf of someone than they are working in their own life, this would be a prime indication that you are over-responsible. If you find yourself over-giving and then getting resentful, this is an unhealthy, out-of-balance dynamic. You must pay very close attention to how you *feel* when interacting with others. Low energy or irritation is a yellow flag. Since we are socialized to be caretakers this is an easy trap to get caught in and a difficult one to get out of. It is a gift to allow someone to trust and step into their self-sufficiency. We may have to cope with guilt: both our own internal guilt over "abandoning" the other person, as well as their attempts to guilt us into staying in the caretaking dynamic. I see this dynamic frequently in all types of combinations, including between spouses. These dynamics are parent-child dynamics and have no place in healthy, long-term adult-to-adult relationships.

2. *Being unconsciously driven by the primal fears of abandonment or engulfment*

When helping clients understand their behaviors in relationships, I often describe the two primal fears we all bring with us when we are born. These are deep within us and activated throughout our lives. As infants, humans are basically little blobs. Unlike some species, we are completely dependent on others for everything we need to survive. We have no teeth or claws, we can't run away and we certainly can't care for ourselves in any way, shape or form. We *instinctively* know this. We know in every fiber of our beings that rejection and abandonment mean certain, very unpleasant death (being eaten, dehydration, starvation or freezing to death: *all bad outcomes)*. We are hard-wired to bond and to avoid abandonment in every way we can. This deep primal fear never leaves us. It is why when someone leaves, it affects us so deeply. It explains why we will tolerate situations that are pretty unpleasant rather than face being 'abandoned' and alone. This is also why social rejection is so painful for us.

Engulfment or entrapment is the second primal fear that we bring with us from birth. The experience of being trapped or unable to move or escape some terrible experience is also an instinctive fear. Most people can readily identify with abandonment, but engulfment or entrapment is less recognizable, though still intense. This primal fear is activated when we feel restricted or controlled, either physically or psychologically. We try to avoid these situations by keeping others at a distance, choosing partners who are cool or distant or even sabotaging relationships when someone gets too close. When clients have ongoing patterns of people abandoning them, even though on the surface it seems counter-intuitive, I would *always* investigate their fear of entrapment as an underlying primal drive.

Since we all have these deep, hard-wired fears, our best strategy is to understand which one is the primary fear most easily activated within us. Which fear is driving us in our relationships? As adults, we can recognize when these are active and deal with them with our mature, higher brain functions.

3. *Unconscious awareness of our family origin patterns and amalgams*

We are deeply imprinted from ages 0-5 and we spend the rest of our lives *reality-testing* what we have experienced and believed about ourselves, the world and our place in it. In trying to make real, lasting change, we have to be aware of the unconscious patterns we carry. An example might be having a sibling born when you were about 2 or 3 years old. While obviously this is a totally common and normal human experience, there could be a pattern that was created and activated that you still follow in your adulthood. So, up until the interloper (new sibling) arriving, you were "little" and then all of a sudden you are now being told that you are the "big girl" and you receive the message that you must now be a big girl (and a good girl). By now having your immediate needs postponed due to the demands of a newborn, you might develop some patterns around that. You might be reinforced and rewarded for not being too bothersome or demanding of mommy, or possibly reprimanded if you assert your needs and desires. Depending on your temperament and personality, you might learn to subvert your needs or get really angry if they are not met. We have to dig a little for these imprinted patterns since they happen before we have development language to store these memories and access them. They are, however, stored in the sensory and body memory.

Patterns are very powerful, but not more powerful than people. We can only change them when we bring them into our conscious awareness, know their source, own them and the impact that the pattern has on our lives and then determine to shift and change the pattern. This is not as easy as one would think. Patterns are like well-worn grooves in our brains that we will access and travel down if we aren't vigilant, sometimes long after we thought we had shifted them. Another key here is that we tend to gravitate towards what is familiar or what we recognize, even if it is unhealthy, because it feels *normal.* That is why we tend to have the same issues in relationships--different places, different faces but same issues underneath. To recognize family of origin patterns, we detail the dynamics and issues of the people who raised us. Often we have picked up and carried those patterns ourselves. An amalgam is an exercise where we might list, for example, all of our male relationships or female and the key dynamics and issues; there are always patterns and themes when we look at the details.

4. *Not taking responsibility for being 'adult' in our relationships*

I have a saying with my therapy clients that an adult can do four things: Manage 1) their time, 2) their money, 3) their emotions and 4) their energy. If *one of these* is missing, one is not an adult--yet. A chatelaine has the keys to the store houses of resources and knows how to manage these wisely to run her estate and her life. This is *all* about focus, intention and using our resources wisely. It is critical that we honestly account for and examine on a regular basis where we are directing our resources. Each resource needs to be *aligned* with our vision and values in our lives.

Time is much harder to honestly account for than you might imagine because it is infused with our energy and emotion as well. For example, if I am doing something I am not enjoying at all, time will seem to drag, while when I am really enjoying myself, it seems to fly by. If work is always on my mind and hanging over my head, I am never really away from it and it seems like I am working more hours because *I am,* mentally in my mind-space. Using the resource of time well means that we get clear on what our priorities are and what is most important. Being hurried, always rushing, running late all the time and not being able to meet what we've committed to creates so much unnecessary angst and anxiety. This is a symptom of not being able to set limits and say "no" to things (and people) that are not in alignment with our vision for our lives and not being honest with ourselves. We deserve to structure our time and efforts so that we can live at a proper pace. As women, the demands for our time are endless, yet time is finite. We must learn to be honest and clear with our priorities and with what matters to us most. This is an ongoing process that we need to keep revisiting over time as our life circumstances and stage of life changes. Faced with a request that I don't want to make time for because it is not in alignment with my vision and values, I remind myself to say, "It's just not a priority for me" rather than, "I don't have time."[4]

Like time, money is something we need to manage well and align where we use it with our values and vision. Emotions, feelings and beliefs are always wrapped up with how we make and spend money. Money is energy and money holds power. Our family of origin and culture imprints us with messages about money, in conscious and unconscious ways. In many families and cultures women are denied access or control over money and this is disempowering (and abusive). The only ways in which we can truly step into our power and own our lives is to master our relationship with money. To address this fully is certainly beyond the scope of a chapter in this book, however there are numerous excellent books that address both the practical aspects of money management (focused on women) and the spiritual dimensions of wealth and abundance.[5]

Women are often in dynamics that are child-parent dynamics. We trade our power, efficacy and agency for affection, for security and *to minimize conflict*. But this keeps us in a constant cycle of feeling like we need *permission* in our lives. We need to honestly

---

4. Laura Vanderkam *https://lauravanderkam.com/* I highly recommend her books and also her 168 hour-week tracking log to take a honest look at how and where we are using our time. I've stopped saying "I don't have time for..." but more accuratel "this is just not a priority"
5. See the further recommended reading list at the end of the book

examine where our dependencies lie. Where do we collapse? Where are we overly reliant on people in ways that compromise our autonomy and independence? Often we convince ourselves that we need to stay in relationships and dynamics because we need certain things, even if there is a very high cost to us emotionally and spiritually.

The other end of this dynamic spectrum is when we are in an inappropriate mothering role for the adults in our lives. We need to know the difference between loving and caring for and *mothering* the adults in our lives, particularly our intimate partners. These are obviously all overlapping aspects of life, but taking an honest inventory of where the imbalances are is critical to be in one's own power. As mentioned in the italics at the start of this chapter, I journaled for *hours, days and years* trying to "fix" my relationship dynamic- only to realize eventually my partner was *unwilling* to make any shifts or changes out of the mother-child dynamic we were living in. It is only looking back that I could see the true cost of this in terms of life and soul energy and what I could have accomplished or enjoyed more with all that wasted energy. The real grief is realizing that we can't suffer enough or sacrifice enough to move another person to want to change. I would encourage taking an honest accounting of relationship dynamics to understand how to manage each of these with clear adult expectations priorities and intentions.

5) *Don't know how to set limits and boundaries appropriately.*

This point comes appropriately after #4 (above) as it is directly related to how we focus our resources. Time, emotion, energy and money are all resources that each one of us has been given. BUT these are *finite.* There are only so many hours in a day, there is only so much emotional and mental energy we can give of ourselves in that day and how and where we spend these *and* our money is a reflection of our clarity on what is important. Where do you say "yes" when your heart is saying "no"? Do you agree to do things because they are planned for off in the future, only to find yourself burdened and resentful when the date arrives? I have learned these lessons the hard way by being a *STAR at the expense of my own life.* What I mean by this is wanting to please others, wanting praise, recognition or a sense of belonging but spending time, emotion, energy and money in ways that didn't support *my own* life-dreams and goals. Even though I having been teaching these ideas for decades, and should practice this better, I have often served other teachers/mentors in their lifes-work and put my own second, third, fourth or last place). For example, I have found myself editing or assisting with *their* book projects - while this manuscript sat all lonely gathering dust in my computer. I've found myself traveling, speaking and teaching to promote the works of others for very little monetary return, and a huge cost in my time and energy.

So, why do we say "yes" when we mean "no"? Because we have been socialized to be *nice*. Nice girls serve others and say "yes" especially to those who we believe are in power and authority. My clients often recognize how strong the pattern of being a 'pleaser & appeaser' is in themselves. What happens when you start saying "NO" ? Guess what? People are pissed because now they need to find someone else to do whatever it is they are requesting of you--but for the most part, they eventually get over it. If they continue to try to bully you or guilt you into doing their bidding, then wish them well and on their way. Remember, we are breaking thousands of years of patterns of appeasement and subverting our power and desires because our lives depended on it. We've been well-trained all of our lives to be 'other-centered' so this is going to take a lot of practice. You will notice that giving *yourself permission* to say *"NO"* is the first step. There will be anticipatory fear and anxiety over the conversation, but then a wave of relief when it is over. Be mindful that then you'll have to cope with the thoughts and feelings regarding why you didn't do this sooner, but this is a further waste of time, energy and emotion. Learn and move on. Know that it does get easier over time and with lots of practice. I like the visual that comes to mind when I think of "iron-clad boundaries." Breaking free of this cage requires an *honest* accounting of how we are using our resources. The journal prompts for this section give guidelines and resources on how to do this.

Yellow flags, soul-killing conversations and journaling

As I am writing this book, I am aware of how often we question ourselves and how others will often make us feel crazy and deny what we are *truly* experiencing. Paying very close attention to how we feel in conversations and in the presence of another person is of utmost importance. When we are journaling our feelings and events, we can become much more aware of patterns, because *there they are* in black and white. (For an example, see the *Instincts* section on *wolf-like dogs*). For me, going back a few months in my journal is a key resource; when I start doubting myself, I can see all the yellow (caution) flags.

One of the clearest signs of needing to let go and move on in a relationship is what I call the *soul-killing conversation*. These are the circular, mental gymnastics-type of conversations about relationship "issues" that go on and on and on and on... and nothing ever gets solved or resolved. They sap your vital soul-energy and are a complete waste of your time. My (new) rule after figuring out over the years that these never solve anything or really make a damn bit of difference in a relationship is: three of these and I am OUT!

Energy does not lie

The clearest indicator of what is happening in relationships is paying close attention to our energy. If you feel drained or irritable around someone that is a clear message that they are siphoning your energy. People don't typically do this consciously (if they *do,* they are more dangerous) but it is up to us to first, become aware that this is happening and, second, stop the flow of energy. When you consciously release and close energy drains you *will* feel very different. This energy is different than *love.* We can cut the cords and flow of energy without severing the love that exists. If you are trying to release the bond you have with someone you are trying to end a relationship with, it is even more important that you use tools to assist you in breaking free.

Cord-Cutting

One of the exercises I do in my own practice as well as with clients is a visualization of spiritual and energetic cord cutting (see the end of this chapter). Additionally, I will use cleansing with sage or other cleansing resins or herbs, Epsom salts and crystals (such as black tourmaline) that I will wear with affirmations to keep myself free of other's energies.

A chatelaine needs to be a good steward of the resources we have and have firm, limits and boundaries. A chatelaine weighs the things people ask of her and responds " I will do this if it aligns with my own priorities, or I can accomplish this with grace and ease for myself." We practice *enlightened self-interest.*

When you can't let go (When a toxic relationship feels like an addition, IT IS)

Very often women get caught up in romantic or other intimate relationships that are malignant and toxic to them but they just can't let go. They *know* that they are suffering. Everyone around them *tells* them they need to end the relationship but they are just not able to completely let go and move on. They feel a cycle of shame around this and it is a very painful cage to be stuck in. I find it most helpful to help women see the relationship from two distinct points of view: first, understanding the brain science on why they can't seem to let go and second, looking at the spiritual dimensions of being unable to let go.

The science of gambling

For a number of years, pathological gambling was considered a compulsive disorder. In the last several years after much debate, the close similarities behind what happens in our brains with substance addition and gambling from a neurological perspective resulted in a shift that now classifies gambling pathology as a type of addiction. In the brain's reward system, intermittent reward is the most powerful way to influence and 'train' an animal (or a person's) behavior.

Behavioral psychologists have known since the early 1950s how to pair learning with rewards and reinforce behaviors. They experimented with caged rats who were given a food pellet every time they pressed a lever. At first the rats pressed the lever randomly or by mistake but they learned really quickly the relationships between the lever and the food reward. Since they could rely on the lever to dispense food whenever they needed it, they had happy rat lives (as happy as they could be in a cage) grooming, playing exercising on a treadmill with the secure knowledge (attachment) that the lever was a predictable source of food reward. This phases was referred to as *continual reinforcement.*

Then in the next part of the experiment, the scientist changed the reward interval to intermittent intervals (*intermittent reinforcement)* and sometimes totally random. The result was that rats responded with frantic lever-pressing. One could say that the some of the rats became obsessed (insecure attachment) with the lever pressing. Some of the rats stopped drinking, grooming and playing and eventually died of dehydration and exhaustion.

During the final phase of the experiment the goal was to completely extinguish the lever-pressing behavior. Extinguishing a behavior means to stop the delivery of reinforcers (in this case the food pellet) that maintains the behavior. So, the rats received no pellets. The rats from the continuous reinforcement group lost interest rather quickly and then preoccupied themselves with other things.

For the rats in the intermittent reinforcement group, the opposite happened. Since the rats had grown accustomed to periods with no reinforcement, they stayed obsessed with the lever, despite receiving nothing. They expected that eventually the reinforcement (lever dispensing the food pellet) would begin again as it had in the past. This created persistence in the face of resistance. Intermittent reinforcement made extinguishing this behavior very, very difficult.

So, what does this mean for getting out of toxic relationships? When a relationship starts, typically there is a lot of reward and positive reinforcement. If you are with a narcissist then you may have experienced "love bombing" literally flooding your brain with dopamine. When positive rewards become intermittent, we can drive ourselves crazy obsessed with trying to get the rewards and positive feelings back again. If the person 'rewards' you once in a while with positive behavior, e.g. kindness or affection, you'll keep going back like the rats who pressed the lever to the point of exhaustion, dehydration and death. This is a form of soul-death.

Loss Aversion

Another neurological factor in gambling addiction (and, in this scenario, difficulty letting go of a relationship that *needs* to end for our physical, emotional, psychological and spiritual well-being) is loss aversion. We want to make up for our losses and "win." We want to be right that all of our self-sacrifice and pain was worth it in the end. We may try and make staying or leaving a values-based decision using the valence of how much *time we've invested* as a mental justification as to why we can't let go. When women find themselves in this mindset, they are willing to spend years in toxic, unhealthy relationships. It is only in the final ending and letting go that they realize their "investment" was actually an investment in poison that was slowly harming every aspect of their being over time. Facing this is very difficult and seems less painful than the ending itself but this is an perverted illusion of the mind.

Endings are death

Humans view endings as death because they are mini-deaths. Because death is associated with deep grief and pain, some of us will avoid endings at all cost. We ghost the men we no longer date or friendships or professional relationships that we no longer want to engage in so we don't have to face the actual endings. Often we will enter into new relationships before the old ones end to soothe ourselves and avoid the pain of endings. But eventually all relationships come to an end.

I find that receiving psychological and or spiritual support through endings is critical to our well-being. In a toxic relationship it is *you* that is dying, just day by day, little by little. You need to trust your inner-knowing and find all of the love and support you need to end the relationship and move on to the love you were meant to live.

The spiritual dimensions of not letting go

Now that you know a little about how our brains get "addicted" to toxic, unhealthy relationships, I wanted to explore the spiritual aspects that might seem a little more esoteric to some. In my life and spiritual journey, I've come to believe that our soul, the very essence of who we are, lives many lives. Souls in general 'stick together', so many people in our most inner-circle of close relationships have been with us before. We are not always in the same roles or genders even, but we do have karma or spiritual business to attend to with the people we are sharing our lifetime with. In my own spiritual work, when I have found relationships very difficult to leave or even understand, I have explored through regression the themes, images or insights that my soul-mind provided so that I could "finish my business" with that soul and move on.

When women I have worked with are unable to move on despite doing the deep psychological work to move forward, my approach would be to understand the ways in which past lives, karma or old debts/contracts may be contaminating or continuing to influence them in not being able to let the relationship go. For example, I worked with a woman who had great guilt over leaving a long-term relationship that really needed to end. In regression she saw this person as her child and she reported that she felt she had abandoned this child in that life-time. We did work on helping her release that old guilt and see that she had already fulfilled her debt and obligation to this person in her current lifetime and that it was now right for her to move on.

Finding a spiritual healer that you trust who has a solid reputation and resonates with you is very helpful in this regard. It is also critically important to listen to your own inner-wisdom with this work. You will recognize and resonate if the information that comes up in a regression is right for your soul's journey. My preference would be to guide the person to access their own images, symbols and experiences coming directly from the deep recesses of their metaphoric mind, but not everyone is able to do that easily without practice. Some healers will connect with a client and recount the images and scenes that they "see." If who they share feels a bit "off", take time to sit with the information for a while and remember that even the most gifted spiritual healers interpret their work through their own lens and experiences.

On Cord-Cutting

For eons spiritual practitioners from all over the world have held that when we interact with others there are literal strings or cord of energy that exist between us. These are largely unconscious and invisible ties but they can affect us in many ways both positively and negatively. The science of quantum physics suggests that the ancients were correct. The fields of energy/alternative medicine also suggest there may be science behind this that we just currently do not understand.

If you are in a long-term or sexually intimate relationship, then even more so. In a sexual relationship regardless of the gender, when one is the receiver - the penetrator is said to have planted a seed of a cord that can draw on the receiver for up to seven years. Energetic cords (called etheric cords) can be attached to the sacral chakra or sexual center or the solar plexus or heart center. I find in my own personal practice that when a relationship is difficult to heal from or release, a ritual of cord cutting is especially helpful. For my clients who are open-minded to this concept, I also share it with them. There is a cord-cutting ritual at the end of the journal prompts. For cutting ties with long term or intense relationships you may want to do this more than once. You know you've done this correctly when you feel *lighter* or relieved and feel less activated by memories, thoughts or interactions with the person.

You have the right to live the best life possible for you. You have the right to live with joy, balance and from the deepest place of your own inner-wisdom. Take the time to quiet and connect with your soul-mind, holding self-love and compassion as you explore.

* If you are afraid to leave a relationship, this indicates a pattern of *abuse*. Abuse takes many forms: physical, emotional, spiritual and financial. If you believe this is your situation, you need the help of a skilled professional and possible legal assistance to leave safely.

Chapter 1
Relationship Cages
Journal Prompts

1. Take a moment to reflect and do an honest accounting of your relationships. Are there relationships that take a lot of your time, emotional energy or other resources?

2. In relationship(s) what unconscious patterns might be at work?

3) Take an honest accounting of how you, as a chatelaine, use your resources:

   a) How well do you manage your money? Do you have enough money to accomplish what is important to you? Do you have enough money to do the things you enjoy in your life? What, if anything, could be better?

   b) How well do your manage your time? Where are the time-drains?

   c) Do you have mastery over your emotions? Where might you be over-invested emotionally?

   d) Do you have enough energy to accomplish the things that are important to you?

4. Where in relationships do you say "yes" when you really want to say "no" or "not now"? What are your fears about setting limits and boundaries?

5. Where might you feel resentment?

6. Is there someone you are waiting on for approval or permission to make a choice or decision?

7. After reflection/journaling, what relationships need to shift and how? Are there any "cages" that you need to get out of NOW? Be on guard for our tendency to just make the cage a bit more comfortable; be bold, be honest   and be brave.

8. Track your dreams or as much as you can remember them upon waking. What are the primary themes in the dreams? What are you doing in the dreams and what are the people around you doing ?

Ritual for Cord-Cutting

When you end a relationship, or if you feel the need to shift the energy dynamics of a relationship, you can cut the cord of attachment (without severing the love that existed). For this work you'll need some quiet time and space where you can do the meditation and then some self-care afterwards to integrate it.

1) *Put yourself in a relaxed meditative state.*

2) *Picture the person you want to cut cords with in front of you.*

3) *Acknowledge any emotions that come up for you, no matter what they are.*

4) *Picture the cords that exist between you; where are they? What do they look like?*

5) *Now, picturing a pair of golden scissors or a large silver knife, cut the cord and say out loud "I cut the etheric energy cord in every dimension of time and space. I return the energy that doesn't belong to me to this person and reclaim what is mine. I cut this cord and heal this place so that there is no longer any flow of energy between us. It is done. It is done. It is DONE"*

6) *After your meditation, drink plenty of water and rest. I also recommend epsom salt bath or cleansing right afterwards. As the water drains, hold the intention of the water being reclaimed and cleansed in the earth.*

7) *If you work with stones or crystals, you can wear those for additional reminders of your work and that you are free and protected from other's energy and negativity.*

The Cage of Self-Abandonment:
Reclaiming Your Power

My high-school guidance counselor told me I was not college material and that I should set my sights more realistically on a trade or technical school. No one in my family had been to college so I didn't have an alternative vision to what this 'expert' counselor told me. I remember driving through Lincoln Park and seeing the big DePaul University sign and wishing from my heart and wondering what it would be like to be a student there. But that was for others; it didn't seem possible at that time for me. It took many years to reality-test, challenge, overcome and far surpass that limitation planted in high school. It has been a very long journey for sure, not only did I attend college (as an adult), I received a master's degree and a Ph.D. Now I am part of the leadership running the college I attended. Miracles DO happen, dreams DO come true, and we should never give up on our hearts desires.

Self-abandonment is the saddest cage of all because we unconsciously create and place ourselves in there. We try and make the cage confortable, we convince ourselves that we are fine in the cage and we contort our bodies, our spirits and our dreams to squeeze into cages that we have clearly outgrown and need to be free from. We believe the lies that people tell us, that limit us.

DePaul Graduation with my son Alex
(1998)

Tenure to Associate Professor with Dean
Marisa Alicea (2016)

Why do we abandon ourselves? First, and most directly the reason is we don't feel worthy of living the life of our dreams. Somewhere along our physical trail we learned that life is supposed to be good *for other people* but that we have a life-is-good ration mindset and that it only gets so good for us. Nothing is further from the truth. Our lives are the direct result of what we focus on and what we allow ourselves to receive. The self-worth block is the one that we need to address first. Once we become crystal clear on what it is that we want, the next elements of the self-abandonment cage are recognizing where we need to clean up the drains on our time, energy and attention and the places where we have totally given our power away.

Related to the self-worth block where we don't believe we can have the lives we dream of, is the belief that we are only worthy if we work really hard and struggle. Our culture really promotes and glorifies this perspective. We *love* the story of the underdog beating all the odds and winning. We *love* to watch people who have been in a really deep hole climb out (and we all clap) even if that hole was one that was self-created. We get tired of fighting, clawing and climbing towards the things we desire and, if we aren't wise in how we steward our time, energy, resources and attention (like a chatelaine) we burn out and run out of gas before we reach our goals.

Over-giving: keeping one's self small as to not threaten our relationships

We don't recognize when others sabotage us for fear that if we are successful that we might outgrow and leave them. Because are afraid of conflict or of losing people's approval, affection or a sense of belonging, we keep ourselves small and the people in our lives send us subtle and sometimes not so subtle messages that there is an acceptable level of growth and expansion and that we must not tread beyond that. We don't *give* our power away, we *trade* it--for love, for approval, for security, and for belonging.

We have to recognize when we have become over-involved in other people's dramas and problems and the way that this drains our soul-energy. I talked about this quite a bit in the previous chapter on relationships, but it is worth repeating here. Not only do we abandon ourselves, we *turn* on ourselves and continue to beat ourselves up and demean ourselves even after others who have done so in our pasts are long dead and gone.

Shame and the self-critic stops us in our tracks and keeps us small. There are two ways that these trickster aspects operate. Shame keeps us feeling unworthy from the standpoint of "you don't deserve XYZ... you aren't good enough, you aren't all that, blah blah blah..." And then, when we actually get over *that* aspect and actually get ready to leave our cages and enter the large arena of life, we put our hand on the door and the self-critic says, "Who do you think you are? To have, be or do_____." These parts of ourselves think that they are keeping us safe by keeping us small and not expanding. But this is an illusion. We must come to terms and to blows and eventual victory over those tricksters within ourselves.

On addiction--Running from the self

There are volumes upon volumes of books on addictions. But I am addressing this here as it is the ultimate form of self-abandonment. *All* addiction can be described as running from the self. Addictions are ways to avoid coming to terms with, and dealing with, ones self, including the woundings and abuse from our past and the woundings and abuse we have dealt to others. Of course as a psychologist, I acknowledge the biological, physiological aspects of addictions to substances such as drugs and alcohol, but it *starts* with wanting to feel better, to numb or to escape ourselves and our psychic, physical or emotional pain. Addiction is a serious cage within the cage of self-abandonment and needs to be dealt with spiritually and therapeutically along with the underlying family of origin issues and psychological pain. A wise teacher of mine once told me that, as long as you are 'underneath the thumb' of *anything* you can't live without, you are in a prison, you are never truly free.

Rewriting our stories - Moving from Victim to Victor

Since the stories we tell ourselves hold so much energy and power, it is imperative that we rewrite our stories to focus on our strengths, gifts and victories to empower and propel us forward. Very often we are in the self-abandonment cage and stay there because we *forget* that we hold the keys to free ourselves and have all along. Journaling is such a powerful tool for life and for change because not only do we process our experiences very differently once we have written them, we can see patterns more clearly and quickly and also be able to draw on all of our past experiences when we feared and were eventually victorious. Energy is released through the hands and through the mouth. When we *write* and change the narrative, it stops all the cycling of that old story and energy that is in our heads. In writing and re-writing our life stories and narratives, it is *key* that we own all of the choices and decisions that we made. We have to be able to see the larger stories of our lives and our roles in all of the chapters. We also need to pay close attention to our verbal stories. At one point on a retreat in Costa Rica in the years following my divorce, I realized how much I was still talking from a victim narrative. As I became more self-aware, it helped me to shift and change in profound ways and be free from that old chapter of my life.

"Anything can happen with a razor"
--Rosanne Roseannadanna

Comedian Gilda Radner had a character on Saturday Night Live in the 70s called Roseanne Roseannadanna who had hilarious commentaries on a variety of scenarios. In one skit she misquoted "everything happens for a reason" as "anything can happen with a razor", which I still laugh about to this day. "Everything happens for a reason" seems a bit fatalistic and not empowering to me. I prefer the stance that *psychologically resilient people make meaning from their experiences.*

"Tomorrowland: where power goes to die."
--Dr. Chelsea Page

Dr. Chelsea Page is a woman I know from a woman's group. She shared this quote in one of our calls and I found it so simple but profound that I asked if I could quote her. "Tomorrowland" quite simply is the putting of our hopes and dreams into 'someday' or tomorrow; it is another form of self-abandonment. It allow us to project our futures outside the cage without taking real action and concrete steps to get out of it.

In 2019, my sister Michele who was 17 months younger than me, passed away from cancer. We looked very much alike and in many ways being with her in her dying was like staring my own death in face. This was transformative for me from the sense that it made me take serious pause about those dreams and desires that I had put into tomorrowland. None of us is guaranteed tomorrow. Your dreams and desires *matter.* Your dreams and desires come from the deepest part of your soul and who you are and you honor your soul and spirit when you put them into motion.

Journal Prompts

1. What were the hopes and dreams of your youth?

2. Which dreams did you pursue? Which dreams died?

3. Think of all the ways you abandon yourself - what are the reasons you do this? (e.g. to avoid conflict? To avoid disapproval or criticism?)

4. Think about the role that your self-critic plays in your life. In what areas of your life is the self-critic most active?

5. Allow yourself to picture living a dream that you have. What emotions or thoughts come up? Record them ALL. Pay particular attention to the ones that imply self-abandonment.

The Cage of Instinct-Injury:
Reclaiming Instinctual Powers

When predators bred in captivity are returned to the wild, their survival has been reported at only around 30%. These animals have been instinct injured and lost many of the skills they need to survive outside of captivity.

In order for us to step into our power and trust ourselves to create the lives we want, we have to be able to hone and trust our instinctual natures. Often women who have not learned to trust their instincts have designed lives on the wishes of others and have lost touch with own their visions, dreams and desires. In my early training I was fortunate to be gifted with Dr. Clarissa Pinkola Estés's book, *Women Who Run With the Wolves.* I still love this book and go back and read sections on a regular basis. It is very dense, rich and full of deep, healing wisdom. One of my dreams is to attend a training or workshop with her in-person. She is a curandera and a storyteller. She describes women as *la loba* (she-wolves) with the essential need to reclaim our wildish natures. She writes about the peril that befalls women when our mothers have failed to teach us to navigate the woods safely. We have dulled our instincts/senses, sight, smell, hearing and intuition, and found ourselves caught in traps. Not only have many of us not learned from our mothers or grandmothers how to access and hone our instincts, but we have also been instinct- injured during our childhoods or adolescence as well. It is *not* their fault either. Often injuries and wounds are multigenerational and our aunties, mothers and grandmothers have had their own woundings. Often the women in our bloodlines lost their instincts and ability to make good choices for themselves. Often they were forced to live marginal lives or worse. If our grandmothers or mothers have not had the opportunity to do their healing work, they certainly don't have the psychic safety and tools to teach their daughters and granddaughters to navigate the woods. When our mothers or grandmothers have not healed or recovered from their instinct injuries, the best advice or wisdom they can give us is to stay away from the woods altogether. This, however, is impossible. When women have been in the *captivity* of cages, like the quote at the start of this chapter, our survival is in danger if we are suddenly released in the 'wild.' To live full lives, to navigate in the world that we are in now, to do the work we came here to do and to make upcoming cultural and social changes, we need to have the skills and confidence to navigate *all* the terrain. We have to keep our eyes open, our ears perked up and our senses alert so that we can recognize traps, cages and predators. I love the notion of healthy women as wolves.

"A healthy woman is much like a wolf: robust, chock-full, strong life force, life-giving, territorially aware, inventive, loyal, roving. Yet, separation from the wildest nature causes a woman's personality to become meager, think, ghostly, spectral. We are not meant to be puny with frail hair and inability to leap up, inability to chase, to birth, to create a life."
--Dr. Clarissa Pinkola Estés,
Women Who Run With the Wolves

Wolf-like Dogs

In addition to my love of horses, I have always had a love and affinity for dogs. I have had many dog companions in my life of all breeds and sizes, but as I was concluding this book and continuing through my journaling process and tracking life-patterns, I recognized a particular pattern with wolf-like dogs as important allies and energies in my own life. In my early 20s while I was living on my own and really expanding my young adult life and having a vision for what I wanted it to be, I acquired an Alaskan Malamute even though my apartment, my budget and my knowledge of dog training at that time were small. I named her Neige (French for "snow"). She was an extraordinary companion and went everywhere with me. I soon learned that she needed much exercise, freedom and room to run. She was a faithful ally and guard especially when I started dating. She pinned more than one suitor to my living room couch with her canines bared. One night, I found a young man I had started dating named John holding her up by her throat in my bathroom trying to choke her. Around that same time I needed to move and was having no luck finding a new rental that would allow me to have her. I found a young man with a farm and a male Malamute and released her to a new home where she would be safe and have lots of room to run, as well as a mate. Despite his promises to keep in touch and let me visit her, I never saw her again. This broke my heart in a million pieces and, although it took a few years, John's violence (he turned out to be an alcoholic) was eventually directed at me; I found myself in a trap/cage.

Many years later, I was working on my Ph.D. and teaching in a Field and Experiential Learning program at a community college. It was a time for visioning and expansion again, thinking about how I wanted my practice and work to take shape, picturing spiritual retreats out in nature (similar to what I am doing now, 20 years later). I felt a strong desire to get another dog, a German Shepard or another Malamute. My son Alex was 10 at the time and able to help walk and care for a new dog. I got a white shepherd and we named her Sasha.

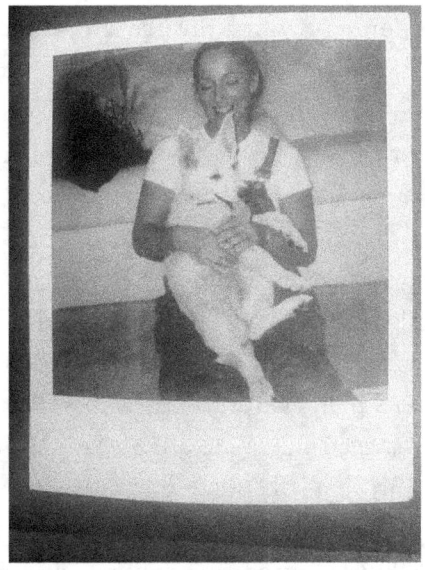

Sasha (Spring 2001)

A year later, she was almost full-grown and I was on a trip to Tamagami in northern Ontario with a group of students doing a retreat. I was in such a good, high vibration and expansive space, really feeling into what I could create when I returned. While I was on the trip, my husband at that time got rid of her, saying that she had bit my son (although my son's version is that they were playing and she accidentally caught him with her tooth). He literally ejected a family member without consultation with me. I never had a say in how to solve for this issue and I never got to say goodbye. This was one of the cruelest things he did during our marriage. He would not allow me my grief or my anger. Looking back now, this should have been a deal-breaker, but I had my son who had already endured my first divorce and my daughter was just a toddler. I somehow put this behind me at the time but I also found myself abandoning my wildish instincts and *back in a trap/cage* that took many more years to extricate myself from.

As I was completing the editing and final touches on this book and again, visioning an expansive future for my work and practice in early Spring 2022, my senior dog Kiki passed away at 14 years old. The previous October, our other dog Wilton who was even older, "crossed the rainbow bridge." My daughter and my family kept sending me pictures of rescues until one day, which happened to be my birthday, a picture of a Siberian Husky-mixed puppy appeared on the rescue site. There was just something about him so we filled out the application to adopt him and went to a meet and greet the following Sunday. I adopted him on the spot. He had been found all alone when he was only a few weeks old and was sick and full of worms and fleas. He was obviously a fighter and very resourceful. Since he was found by the side of a road, we named him Larue.

Interestingly enough, I had been experiencing distress and the feeling of being trapped and drained in a relationship with a man I had been seeing the last six months. His jealous, angry, negative response to my adopting the dog was the final evidence I needed to end the relationship. I journaled "What *is it* about me and dogs and the men in my life?" This was the third time this had happened with issues with wolf-like dogs and the men I was involved with (I know I'm slow, I needed this lesson three times). It finally dawned on me that there was a relationship between my visions for freedom and expansion and specifically *wolf-like* dogs. Embodying the energy of *la loba*, the she-wolf, I believe I am drawn to these dogs as a clue for listening and honing my own wildish nature, my own truest instincts.

"Gotcha Day" for new adopted puppy, Larue

In terms of therapy work with instincts and animals, my *direct* experience is with horses. Here, I will focus on the ways in which horses can also provide wisdom and instruction on reclaiming our instincts and divine feminine power.

Instinct, horses and the divine feminine

I have had a lifelong affinity (some might say obsession) with horses. When I was a very small girl I went to visit some relatives that had horses. I asked my mother to put my hair in a ponytail because I didn't want the horses to know I was a human. Decades later, I was lying down, having healing work done by a Shaman. He shared that during the healing, when he looked at my feet, he saw horse hooves.

The saddest times in my life were when I didn't have horses. My first husband literally made my life miserable and unbearable until I agreed to sell my beloved mare named Megan Point, "Maggie" who I had raised and trained since she was 3. Interestingly that mare would not let him get within a few feet of him--ever. Whenever he approached, she barred her teeth; she was desperately trying tell me what kind of human he was! My second husband was warned when we started dating: "I am a horsewoman, I will always be a horsewoman and, if you can't deal with that, don't be with me." And again, as this relationship went on, I found myself in another situation of having to defend having horses in my life and defending them in my daughter's life as well. I had made a commitment that I would never allow the question of having horses on the table for discussion. This second time, however, I knew better.

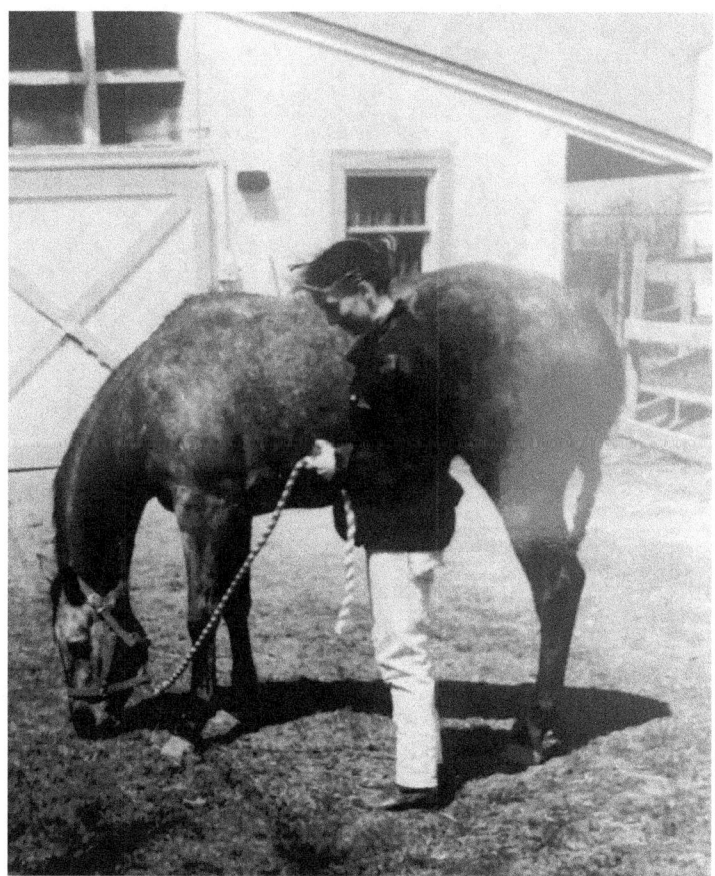

My first horse, Maggie (1990)

Horses embody the divine feminine. They have been excellent teachers and mentors for me, my students and my clients helping us to get in touch with our instincts, set limits and boundaries and honor our nature.

Just south of a town called Uffington in England is a three-thousand-year-old white chalk effigy of a stylized horse that is best seen from the air. This is believed to be an image of the Goddess Epona, a central Celtic Goddess. In 2011, while presenting at a conference on animal-human relationships, I met Welsh equine ethologist Lucy Rees, who, after conference hours, shared the long and detailed legend of Epona over pints in a local pub. She said, "It was recorded in ancient times, and it was ancient then." Epona represents the divine feminine, a time when women and the feminine were honored, respected and free. In some cultures, Epona was (and is) a psychopomp with a deep connection to other realms of knowing- bridging the world of the seen and unseen, the living and the dead. Similar to the fate of other Goddesses in history, her value as a spiritual icon and symbol and surrounding mythology were denigrated by patriarchal religious values. It is no accident that women and girls are so strongly drawn to horses at this time in history where the world is in desperate need of reclaiming the divine feminine.[6]

Epona as the horse goddess and symbol of the divine feminine was usurped but many ancient aspects of Epona remain. Horsemen from Gaul (which is now modern France) who were conscripted in the Roman conquest brought the worship of Epona to Rome, where she had her own holiday (December 18) as a goddess of war. Previously, Epona is known to have been widely revered as a protector of horses, cattle, donkeys and oxen. Until the Christian era, roses were used to decorate both horses and stables to honor Epona. Interestingly, in contemporary times, the Kentucky Derby made roses the official flower for the derby in 1904. It is also called the "Run for the Roses." Because of horses' critical role in warfare, and Epona's role mediating between the lands of the living and the dead, the devotion to Epona became linked to the winning of wars. The idea of Epona as a war goddess is repugnant from the standpoint of the divine feminine, though it makes sense that a mother may have prayed to Epona as a strong feminine figure to protect her sons and their horses fighting in faraway lands.

Horses were once essential to our lives as modes of transportation. More than any other animal, horses have had an enormous impact on human cultures throughout history.

6. Green, M. (1991). Women and goddesses in the Celtic world. *Journal of Contemporary Religion*, 6(3), 4-8.

They have historically carried us in every aspect of our lives, into warfare and to the grave. In modern life, they are seen as romanticized luxuries from an era gone by, as well as a symbol of wealth.

I now understand my deep connection with horses as a symbol or embodiment of the divine feminine. It is no accident that women all over the world go to great lengths and expense to find connections with horses. In my decades of work with horses, despite more than 6,000 years of domestication, they seem to retain much of their natural instincts. I have met severely traumatized/abused horses who have literally shutdown all but their most basic responses to survive but this, in my experience, is rare. There are a number of innate qualities horses possess that can teach women to access, hone and honor our instincts.

Horses are prey animals. They are food for other predators (including humans). As such they have a highly developed awareness for their environments. They are especially attuned to any subtle changes in their environments and to energy around them. They maintain their instincts and balance if allowed plenty of time outside and in community with their herd-mates. Horses are especially nervous about being trapped with no place to escape or exit. Freedom (and freedom of movement) is most important to horses. When they are frightened, they typically run first and ask questions later (once they are at a safe distance). For my daughter and myself the greatest moments of joy are when we turn our horses out on our pastures and they run and buck and leap with such enthusiasm (before just hanging out and eating all day). Women, like horses need freedom and the ability to move with enthusiasm. My horses have taught me to listen to my most basic fear response, take "flight" or get some distance so that I can observe and collect more information and to be particularly mindful about knowing exits and paths to escape if and when necessary.

On intent and congruence

One of the areas of instinct and intuition that we need to hone is recognizing intent and congruence or incongruence. Horses as prey animals are very adept at this as it is essential for their survival. *Predator* behavior is incongruent. An example I often give clients is in the behavior of my barn cats. They will be resting (pretending) until a mouse gets a little too close - and then spring into action and capture the creature unaware. Human beings have elevated incongruence to a high art called "acting"- although the *best* actors are the ones who are actually energetically feeling or experiencing what they are portraying in their roles. I have found my horses to be very reactive - not to negative feeling states necessarily, but rather when a visitor (client or otherwise) is 'acting' one way but actually feeling another. They are excellent BS detectors. My mare Savannah was the *best* at this - particularly with men. She *demanded* congruence and that people be "right" or in alignment with their energy before she would let them get close to her. When we've allowed ourselves to be duped or victimized by a predator, we can typically look back and track all of the places where we ignored our instincts and the little 'red flags' of incongruence; the upturned corner of the mouth where a smile was actually a *smirk*, the clench of a jaw, the narrowing of the pupils, eye contact that was too intense or avoidant, body tension, shifts in breathing, and changes in proxemics, for example.

We are the only species that ignores our basic instinctual responses.[7] Women especially do this because of social conditioning to be "nice" or pro-social and because we overly rely on verbal rather than non-verbal (more accurate) cues. Being with my horses has taught me to pay more attention to energy and the non-verbal and to more fully trust my feelings and reactions. One of the ways that we rekindle our connection to our instincts is by honoring and trusting them in everyday situations- so that we can fully trust them in more high-stakes scenarios. Developing a high-degree of intuition, emotional self-awareness, scanning the body for signals and trusting our body-wisdom are all essential in developing our instincts. Regularly asking and assessing "what does my body need right this moment?"--and most importantly honoring those needs--is an important path to connection.

---

7. I highly recommend De Becker, G., & Stechschulte, T. (2000). *The gift of fear*. Recorded Books.for reading about and understanding the role instincts in keeping us safe from violence.

Assessing others' energy

When someone enters my barn, my horses begin the process of assessing them and 'measuring' them. They are reading energy, behavior, voice and emotion. They are taking in this data and deciding how they will adjust their own behaviors based on what they are receiving. Because they aren't bogged down by our spoken language and social conventions, they rely on their instincts, nonverbal cues and intuitive senses. As humans we've been doing this since we were infants, before we too were bogged down with language and *trained* to respond in certain ways by our caregivers and our culture. We never entirely lose this ability to read energy and subtle non-verbal cues and tone, which is how we often have a 'gut' instinct that someone is lying to us for example, but we mostly just talk ourselves out of our intuition or ignore the messages. The energy of others affects us--whether we are consciously aware of it or not. When you encounter someone, a friend or stranger, slow down your breathing and try and get a sense of what their state and energy pattern is. Emotionally, how does this person *feel* to you? A really good practice is to pay very close attention to any involuntary contractions in your muscles - this is typically an initial fear response. Once you are alert to how other's energy feels to you, you have to train yourself to keep it from affecting you. Those of us doing healing work in the world, must absolutely know how to release what does not belong to us- or we will burn ourselves out.

Present moment awareness

One of the greatest gifts of horses is the ability to be in present moment awareness. Horses are simultaneously vigilant to all that is going on around them and relaxed. The have mastered vigilance without angst. When something frightens my horses they react (sometimes quite explosively) but then they literally shake it off, through their whole spines, blow out their accumulated energy and breath and then return to baseline. Healthy horses, like healthy women, are able to *mostly* let go and not hold on to their frightening or painful experiences because they trust their present-moment awareness and instinctual responses to keep them safe from future threats. They do *learn*, very quickly of course, but unless they are traumatized*[8] they can usually cope with a range of challenges and experiences. It is essential that they have access to time in nature and with each other for this release and rebalancing to occur. Unlike us, they have memories of the past and expect a future, but they don't *live* there in their minds.

As women, we tend to do a lot of what I call *time travel*, where we are ruminating on the past or stressing about the future and having real, physiological responses to those things that exist in our only in our minds. Fighting these imaginary 'tigers' (threats in our minds) takes an enormous toll on our bodies, minds and spirit as if we were fighting actual tigers. The goals of most healing modalities in psychotherapy is cultivating calm, present-moment awareness, because this is when the

---

8. *I reference more on trauma at the end of this chapter

healing insights, new perspectives, forgiveness, revelations or intuitions enter us. Often just allowing ourselves to enter the present moment, and asking, "What do I see? What do I hear? What do I smell? What do I feel? Where am I?" can be a revelation and healing of instincts for many of us.

Present moment awareness of our environment is the key to safety in all situations. People who work around horses everyday often get hurt because we become too relaxed, sloppy or less-mindful in their presence than those who are more vigilant due to the novelty of the situation. I have in my clinical work observed many clients (children, adolescents and adults) who freeze and wait for instruction or *permission* to keep themselves safe. For example, I brought a group into the arena once and the horses became highly activated. One woman said "These horses have issues!" (It was the group with the issues by the way; the horses, who prior to this were their normal selves, were just reacting to all the energy and dynamics in this group). Then, another member of the group who was frightened (justifiably so) by three loose, highly activated horses in a shared space said, "Okay, now we are all in danger."

My response was, "Then what are you waiting for? What do you need to do right now to feel safe? Get to somewhere where you feel more safe!" (Like outside the gate). This was a good lesson for this group of mostly women to 1) notice how they were feeling, 2) own how they were feeling and 3) act on those feelings without waiting for permission.

Groundedness and connection to nature

Like horses, women are deeply connected to the natural world. Our bodies and our energies are affected by the seasons, the moon and the weather throughout our lives. To be balanced and healthy, horses need to spend most of their time outdoors. Women too need time in nature to connect with the earth's energy, to ground ourselves, to experience sun, sky, wind and weather. One of my teachers believed that we have to spend a minimum of one hour outside everyday-just to survive. To thrive - we need much, much more. In our contemporary lives, we spend large amounts of time in *man-made,* artificial environments. This literally cuts us off from our primal source of energy, rebalancing and renewal.

Clients often ask me what 'grounding' means. I use it as literally directing one's energy *into the ground* as well as slowing down our energy. When we are over-activated, have excess energies or are unfocused and out of alignment with our bodies, putting our selves on the earth and breathing and directly sending energy into the ground is curative. If we find ourselves unable to go out and put our feet on the earth because we are in an urban or indoor environment, holding stones or crystals can be grounding. Handling clay or working with our hands can also help ground us. Clients often ask me how often they should practice grounding themselves. My response is: do it so often that it becomes automatic so that grounded-awareness is your most comfortable, natural state.

Energy, boundaries and communication

Have you ever watched a film of a herd of horses running at full speed and wondered how they don't run into each other? Additionally, they are all 'linked' in their consciousness to the leader of the herd and they are all headed in the direction the leader is going. From the time horses are born, they learn to fully feel and experience the energetic field that exists around them (and all living things). The mares and other adults in their herd teach them appropriate respect and boundaries. They each have bubbles of energy around them and they can sense and feel them- which is how they can run without crashing into each other. Mares are really adept at teaching their youngsters all of the boundaries and customs of horse culture. They learn to live in a herd family dynamic for the survival and benefit of all. Like so many other aspects of life that have been turned upside down by toxic masculinity and patriarchal culture, horse culture has been impacted as well. Mares, if left to their own natural devices, would never choose a stallion who did not exercise restraint and control, as the opposite of those behaviors would be a threat to survival of the herd. Throughout time however, men have bred 'hot blooded' stallions, whose very qualities are reflections of themselves. Mares (the divine feminine) are typically the leaders of the herd with the stallion following behind offering protection.

Horses develop and learn spacial and physical-body boundaries from their mares and herdmates. These are constantly reinforced through non-verbal communication. When a horses approaches another horse, there is either permission to come in closer, or a warning to not advance any further. If the first non-verbal warning is ignored, the result is typically a swift squeal, bite (or threat to bite) or a kick (or threat to kick).

Physical boundaries are critically important for women and girls. I am still amazed that, in our current time and culture, women don't fully own their bodies and feel like we can say, "NO". This is a huge problem for us on many levels. I had a woman in her mid-life with lots of previous horse experience, come to the barn for a session one beautiful fall day. One of my geldings, who literally has no boundaries (and hence is *really* good at teaching people and other horses to set them) went up to her uninvited and nuzzled her ears, face and hair as she literally stood frozen with this unpleasant look on her face. I asked her, "Are you okay with him doing that?"

"No," she responded.

"Then what is it going to take for you to make that clear to him?"

Was she waiting for permission? Did she not want to hurt his *feelings?* Probably both. This response is all too common in many girls and women. Men we don't know feel that they can touch us without our permission or hug us when they barely know us. This can be a subtle way of saying they own us and our bodies. Women often let men touch them or hug them even when it makes them very uncomfortable because we don't want to be perceived as 'not nice.' It took me years to learn to set strong physical boundaries. At the end of a spiritual workshop I was co-leading, a man I had never met before asked if he could hug me, and I said "no". At least he *asked*, but the shocked look on his face at my response told me it was pro forma rather than a genuine request for permission. I am not against hugging, just against us doing so when we feel obligated to say "okay" when we really want to say no or when the energy we are experiencing repels us from that type of close contact with someone. My mare Savannah taught me this. She was very selective about who could touch her, and when, especially her face. It didn't mean she didn't like someone; she was just very particular about having people in her space and touching her. There were times she could be affectionate and cuddly, but it was *always* on her terms. Now I am crystal clear on my physical space.

"Manage your energy..."

My mare Savannah was a very tolerant mare and a excellent therapy horse. She did, however, hold me to a higher standard in terms of the emotion and energy I brought into any situation because she knew I was capable of managing myself. Early one morning I was in a very foul mood when I entered her stall. She pinned her ears back and lifted her lip and snapped (bit) in the air in my general direction. I started having a meltdown, crying and saying, "Me? Really? You're pinning your ears at ME? I'm your PERSON! I love you! I take care of you!"

Then, to make a point, I slammed her stall door and accidentally slammed my finger in the door. After icing my finger and sobbing for about 20 minutes back in my car, I breathed myself back together and reentered her stall and she was like, "Oh, good morning, you... manage your energy before you come into my space." She was such a great teacher.

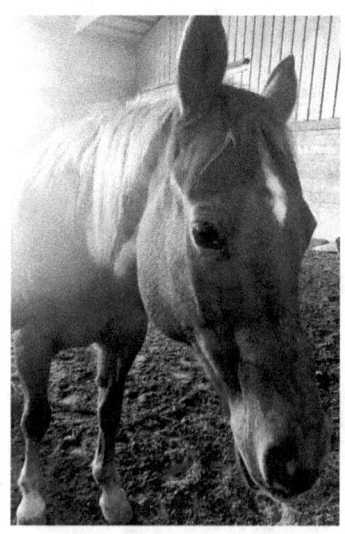

Savannah (2017)

Dangling the Golden Carrot

Because my horses honor their instincts, it is difficult (almost impossible) to trick them and convince them that someone is safe and okay when they have decided not to trust them. Human women on the other hand are often easily fooled and tricked by a golden carrot. When women have fallen prey to a toxic, unhealthy predator, an important area of exploration for us is: what is the doorway for the predator? How and why did you ignore your instincts and 'red flags?' If we are to navigate safely in the world we need to know our vulnerabilities and where we are susceptible. Predatory people have really well-honed people-reading skills and they use our vulnerability against us. For example, they may recognize how we want others to see us and reflect that to us in ways that initially make us feel seen and validated. They may use flattery and compliments or give us that which we long for most in relationships. But in a relationship with a predator, this is just bait to get us into the cage. We can all fall prey and into this cage, but it is crucial that we learn from the experience and don't repeat the same mistakes again. Once a woman is clear on her susceptibility to future predators and traps, then her work is self-forgiveness. Forgiving ourselves is the thing that restores our intuitive nature.

We often believe that the male predators in their lives are responsible for the denigration and dismantling of our lives. While that is true, we also need to be aware and deal with our own inner predator in our psyche who concurred. A woman's true and wildest nature is the part of us that balances the inner predator within.

"People show you who they are. Believe them"

One of my teachers, Angelis Arrien, used to say, "Arieahn, people show you who they are...believe them" and I now say this often. When we hold out hope that someone is a good human being deep down somewhere inside, despite all evidence to the contrary, this is more about *us* projecting our light and our goodness *on* to them. Women tend to do this *a lot*, especially if we are called to be healers in the world. When we are doing healing work part of our training is to look for strengths and positive qualities to build on. In intimate personal and business relationships this can be a disaster. I now hold a three-strike rule (like in baseball), however, if the first transgression is grave enough, there are no second chances. My Indian father never gave up on anyone, but he did figure out that he could hold out hope for the person's growth and transformation while, at the same time, not keeping them in his inner-circle. We have to be honest with ourselves about the cost of betrayals and toxicity and this is part of instinctual awareness. Often we have become so accustomed and numbed to pain that we don't realize how much we suffered until we are actually free.

As a healer in the world, I have found it helpful to think of people as having a Self (capital "S") representing the *soul* that they are in the world which is divine, eternal and worthy of our love and compassion. We also have a self (small "s") which is the ego self--which is transitory, illusory and often the toxic, harmful, unevolved part the personality that is running the show. You can love the soul ("S") of a person, and chose not to engage in a relationship with the personality and identity ("s") that they have in this lifetime.

Co-opting the unhealthy masculine

One pattern I've begun to discern and discover is the ways in which women who are high achievers professionally co-opt unhealthy masculine patterns on an unconscious level. When I examine my trajectory in my 20s and 30s, I can look back at all the ways in which I unconsciously took on these behaviors and patterns, thinking that was what I needed to do to be successful. I notice that I did this in parenting as well. Without strong, healthy fathers, I tried to be *both* mother and father to my children. Often when I was afraid, my default approach was male-authoritarian and ultimately a disaster. What I have had to learn over time is to recognize the high costs of this to my body, spirit, soul and relationships and that I needed to seek out women who could exemplify and model feminine strength and leadership. This can be a whole chapter or book in and of itself!

Being a good soldier - almost losing my vision

Learning to trust and most importantly, act on, our instincts is a lifelong learning process. We've had years and multiple generations of having to tolerate cages. I *still* have to practice awareness of my instinctual responses as well as continually monitor my willingness to act on those responses.

I served for a number of years in a support role in a healing collective. I had a number of powerful learning and healing experiences as a part of that group work, but had begun, after five years or so, to hold a new vision for my work and life that would mean letting go of that service to the group in order to make space do my own work in the world. Early in the morning before one of our gatherings I accidentally injured my right eye. The pain was excruciating and I think I was in shock and a little out of my body. One of my team-mates took me to buy eye drops and a bag of frozen peas to put on my eye. The absolutely insane part of this story is I served that day in the workshop. All day. I participated in all the activities and led a smudging ceremony and sang a traditional song for the group. I did have a very powerful meditation journey myself (probably because I was already out of my body and, due to the pain, somewhat out of my mind. At the end of the day, the group's leader had my colleagues (finally) take me to the ER. The injury was severe and the doctor who examined my was in disbelief about how long I waited to come to the ER. I ended up having to be treated every day for 10 days, wore a patch on my eye with special ointment and meds and was blind in that eye for several weeks. The doctors were not sure I would regain my vision at all.

I almost lost my VISION. I almost lost my vision. I almost lost my vision!

What haunts me still is why I soldiered on that day? What sense of duty or obligation made me stay? This was not a matter or life or death or survival. This was just a workshop, one of many, and I wasn't even leading it...just supporting. Why didn't I insist and advocate--or *demand* for myself? I could blame the group's leader for not giving me permission to leave immediately- but then this would not have been the powerful lesson I am sharing here. This is clearly an area of my own work that I need to be vigilant about. I was raised and acculturated to tolerate a lot without complaint. As I am doing this work at this point in my life, I am holding this experience uppermost in my mind. I am also holding the mottos: 1) Tolerate Nothing. 2) Do not abandon your vision for anyone, for any reason.

And On Trauma

As mentioned earlier, horses that have been severely abused or traumatized become dull to their instinctual natures and seem dissociated. I have fortunately rarely met horses like this but I mention this here because I want to recognize that women can also suffer from deep trauma and this requires expert trauma-focused therapy to resolve. Trauma is a fear response that has become "stuck" neurologically and, when the fear response gets activated, the person experiences the full response without resolution and a return to safety and emotional baseline. In my experience, somatic experiencing and taking both a top down and bottom up approach has had the most benefit in resolving the trauma response.[9] The suggestions in the chapter are still applicable and helpful once the more serious symptoms have been addressed and treated.

Journal Prompts

1. What is the role of instincts in my life currently? Where are you 'shut down' or numb to your instincts ?

2. Where in your life were you instinct injured? Have you healed these injuries? Have you forgiven yourself if necessary?

9. See Van der Kolk, B. (2014). The body keeps the score: Brain, mind, and body in the healing of trauma. *New York.*

Levine, P. (2012). Somatic experiencing.

3. When was a time you trusted your instincts? What was the outcome?

4. When was a time you ignored your instincts, yellow and red flags? What was the outcome ?

5. Track your dreams or as much as you can remember them upon waking. What are the primary themes in the dreams? What are you doing in the dreams and what are the people around you doing ?

The Cage of Ashes (and Shit):
Clear Your Hearth

"She's mad,
But she's magic.
There's no lie in her fire."
--Charles Bukowski

I had been working two or three jobs since I was pregnant with my second child, my daughter. Working multiple jobs, pursuing my doctorate and licensure, raising the kids and running a household left me barely running on fumes. I was often too exhausted to feel angry and resentful at how imbalanced my life had become. There was no fuel for fire or passion of any kind.

I was walking toward the grade school to pick up my little daughter one day. There was a grassy knoll outside the entrance to the building. I had this thought: "I'm so exhausted ... I'm just so tired...I'd like to lay down there on that grass for just a few minutes. That would be sooooo good...Would anyone think it was weird if I just took a little rest there before the kids come out?"

Even scarier, I found myself at a train stop one day imagining driving my car around a railroad crossing when a train was approaching, thinking "Well, that would be terrible...but at least I would get some rest." This was not living--this was just not dying.

As a clinician, it felt really risky to write this (above) being so candid about how exhausted I was at this point in my journey. But it was, and is, the truth. Before we can restart and re-spark the passion and energy in our lives, we have to take the time to rest, heal and reclaim our energy and our power. Exhaustion and imbalance is a cage within a cage. We live in a culture that often cultivates martyrdome. The truth is, there is no nobility in living an unbalanced life. It shows a complete and total disconnection from the needs of the body and lack of awareness of a number of spiritual principles.

Inspiration instead of desperation

When was the last time you were *truly* inspired? When did you last feel that tingly, heart-beating-fast feeling? When have you last felt that energized, can't sleep feeling? the kind of energy that is almost *super*natural feeling? Where are you and your heart on *fire?* How often do you do things that tap into and feed your creative spirit?

Does your life feel like you are living from crisis to another crisis? Are you too exhausted to do anything other than what is absolutely necessary? Has your life become a grind? I knew I was in trouble when I found myself constantly saying "I'm exhausted." I said it so much my kids picked it up and started saying it all the time as well. Also I found myself living for some future more balanced version of me. I constantly journaled, "As soon as I ...(finish climbing whatever mountainous situation I was facing at the time) then I can can relax, or have fun or pursue my heart's desire." When one writes that in one's journal for *years* we start to realize this is a *lifestyle*, not some temporary situation with set end-point.

This cage is one of the most difficult to recognize for several reasons. First of all, none of us would willingly enter a cage of ashes and shit. This cage happens slowly over time while we are distracted and driven if we are not vigilant and protective of tending to our energy and creative fires. It sneaks up on us. As women, we are socialized to meet the needs of everyone else *first*, then what ever is left over (if there is any energy left) is ours. Second, we live in a bizarre, somewhat pathologic culture in which the mainstream does not value the creative spirit as an essential part of healthy adult living. Singing, dancing, art and creativity are the realm of children and 'professionals'. If anyone has criticized our creations along our trail, we often lose our enthusiasm as a form of self-protection from criticism. Third, our creative energies may go into creating physical life (our children) but over time we forget that this very same creative energy and impulse resides in us at *every* stage of the lifespan. And fourth, we often do not recognize the differences between anxiety and excitement and we sometimes unconsciously accept crisis as a substitute for passion because it makes us feel alive. Creative fire is essential to a vibrant, healthy life at every stage of our lifespan.

The state of our creative fires

Women, by *nature,* are creators. My Indian father Greg called women "givers of life." We have the capacity to create new life in our bodies. Whether we *choose* to become birth-mothers or not, this energy is within us, to *create*. If we can not create children in our bodies for whatever reason we still have access to that creative life-force energy. Sometimes this creative impulse can be stifled or snuffed out because we are also socialized to please and be "good" girls and women. One of the quickest ways to kill eros and the creative impulse is through shame, self-consciousness and fear of judgement or criticism. Typically all that it takes to put out our fire is for a critical teacher, parent or friend to stop us in our tracks, and then our self-critic picks up the task from there. We often look to our lovers or mates for passion, without recognizing that there is also another place for this energy in a fire that we alone are responsible for tending. I find it interesting that patriarchal religions that have sought to control women's energy and power all use shame, *especially* sexual shame, as the main weapon in their arsenal. This is explored in greater detail in a later section.

As adolescents, we are full of creative energy. It manifests in a number of ways including intense sexual energy, idealism and rebellion. It is *set the world on fire* energy. Their disdain for older adults and rage at having to enter the adult world (and their perception of us as 'boring') has some merit and validity to it. Although not always consciously, they can see that for many of us, our fires are barely embers if they exist at all. On some deep unconscious level they see our ashes and our shit and they resist for as long as they are able the tidal pull into a world that seems to be no fun at all.

Fear of getting burned

One of the primary emotions we need to face during all change and transformation is fear. There are plenty of myths and cultural stories about passion and fire getting out of control with dire consequences. Also we *are* descendants of women who got burned, literally, at the stake for being visionaries, midwives, healers or defying social convention of the time. In our collective soul-memory as women, we carry these memories. Is it any wonder we are cautious of fire? Women with vision, passion and power are often targeted.

Fires turned to ashes

How then, do our creative fires turn to ashes? A fire is a living energy, not a thing. It requires a balance of oxygen, fuel, heat and a chemical chain reaction. The creative alchemy that happens when an idea ignites in us is the first spark in lighting the fire. We must provide it with fuel and oxygen in order for it to grow from a small flame to a full-blown fire. Sometimes, before it even has a chance, we don't have the room to breathe (oxygen) nor the energy (fuel) to feed it. A balanced fire provides warmth and comfort, cooks our food and is the metaphoric center of our beings. Our sun, the ultimate fire, is essential for life on our planet. Our own creative and soul-fires are essential for our lives as well.

Fuel first.

As I wrote previously in *Relationship Cages,* the demands of women's lives are *infinite.* As women, we are well-trained and socialized from toddlerhood to meet the demands of everyone around us. God help us if we are "big" sisters when we are in truth really little, and are trained to be quiet about our own needs and are *'good girls'* when we *'help mommy with the new baby.'* One of the worst insults you can hurl at a woman is to call her "selfish." Most often, we try our damndest to be stars in our lives but usually this is at our own expense. I often hear from women in my practice that their lives are dominated by meeting the demands and problem solving for everyone in their families. This is a terrible predicament. Our time and energy is finite. If we are not selective sifters of where to direct our time and energy, we will find ourselves depleted to the point of utter exhaustion. When I talk about creativity, inspiration or fun, typically my female clients look at me like I'm completely disconnected from reality. In a sense, I am; the reality of their lives is there is simply no time or space for anything other than work, work, work and caring for everyone. I continually practice 'reality testing' at this stage of my life. I am trying to find and offer my clients another perspective and the notion that there is another way.

I *do remember.* I know when I was in a similar place in my own life, when someone would suggest *anything* else I needed to add to what I was already doing, I wanted to punch them in the face. I was, literally, "burned out." The anger and rage many women express in my office is fueled by resentment, a deep knowing that their fires have gone cold.

Often our own fires are burnt out and all that we have are the ashes of cold-dead fires from our youth. We don't even have a sense of where to begin to reignite or draw fuel from, but, probably more importantly, we don't even realize that it is not only possible to have a fire our their lives; it is absolutely essential. Our lives are dictated so much by the incessant demands of others that there is little time or energy for anything other than the essentials: work and then collapse. This is a difficult cage to get out of. Its primary symptom is exhaustion. Getting free from this cage requires an engaging of the will, the heart and the mind. We can restart a fire with a tiny spark if we can get some of the other conditions aligned. There are many stories of nomadic or migratory people taking embers from their fires with them to new places. I love this image that we can move our embers to start new fires wherever we travel. Likewise, perhaps we can gift embers to those who may need them or borrow embers from those who have healthy fires going to restart our fires when they've gone cold.

Before you try and restart your fire, some general scullery work is required. You must sweep out the old ashes to make a new fire. Additionally, you will need to learn to set limits and boundaries around what you are willing to take on on behalf of others. Your dreams are worthy and important but you *must* make them priorities. No one else can or will do this for you. You must learn to say "No" or "Not now."

So before we can rekindle or re-spark our fires, we need to have fuel. This essential first step and how long it takes will depend on how empty one's 'energy tank' is at this point. If you find yourself completely exhausted and unable to even consider creativity or inspiration, then a radical break is needed. Often women's bodies, in their wisdom, will accomplish this by creating an illness or a health crisis to stop us and make us refuel. Instead of a health crisis, however you can consciously choose to withdraw from everything except the most essential functions and make extreme self-care a priority.

Often when women have had a big loss or heartbreak in their lives, I use the metaphor of "open-heart surgery" with them.

"If you just had open-heart surgery, or major injury/wound to your physical heart, how would you approach recovery?"

Each woman should have her own process and ideas for what self-care looks like; we make a list and then commit to a timeframe for self-care and gradual reentry into all responsibilities after, of course, taking an inventory and accounting of what needs to go! A weekend is *not* enough - it's a good kick-start, but depending on the level of burn-out it may take a few months of extreme self-care for a women to refuel and find the energy to move forward in her life. Be careful of thoughts (or people) who try to tell you that self-care is selfish. It is not. It is loving and it is wise. It will allow you to heal, to open and be more loving to others rather than being needy, resentful or manipulative. Additionally, you will need to deal with the faulty belief that if you stop to rest and take self-care that your life will unravel.

This is not just about a spiritual and mental break. The body needs support as well. Nutrition, supplements and lots of sleep and rest are essential. Working with a holistic physician or practitioner is very helpful for advice and guidance in this healing (refueling) process. If the people in your life are not willing to support you in the need for spiritual and physical recovery, that in itself is a major red-flag and issue to be addressed and remedied.

Clean up your Shit (and get rid of the responsibility for everyone else's)

As of this writing, I have at home, 3 horses, 2 dogs and 4 barn cats. I love living together with all these creatures, however this also means *I clean up a lot of shit.* I've developed a saying for the 2-leggeds around me: "I clean up a lot of shit every day. I'm not willing to clean up yours too!" I've also noticed that mucking stalls is a good fitness routine, but even more oddly, some of my best solutions to problems or most inspired ideas come when I am cleaning up horse shit!

On this journey, you are going to want to start with with a clean hearth and as little clutter and baggage as possible. For most of us, this requires major clean up. There is no judgment here. As I wrote earlier, this aspect of the cage sneaks up on us. We are exhausted and things tend to pile up and get out of hand. There is a reason why I recommended self-care and refueling above as this next step requires energy, commitment and focus. This is a critical step on your journey that you should take seriously and not skip, even if you feel resistance. This is about making space energetically for your new life and your dreams. All of the major spiritual traditions teach simplicity and order. You don't have to live in the austere conditions of a monk. However, being organized is the result of having clear intent and priorities, as well as trust and faith that you can always manifest anything you need at anytime. Women who live frantic, dramatic, disorganized chaotic lives have low levels of self-awareness because this kind of life creates so much emotional anxiety and distraction from our intuitive selves.

Start with your physical space: "As within, so without"

When I start on a big project or presentation, I *have* to clean off my desk first. While this may look like procrastination, I understand that energetically I am doing psychic preparation. It is really important to have environmental (outer) order to support inner-order and focus. Your physical surroundings should reflect balance, order and organization. All the things in our environment require our attention and energy. When you are living with broken things, accumulations of old, unnecessary or useless things and disorganization, your attention and emotional energy is being squandered.

For example, after my mother passed away, I had a number of items from her apartment in a box. I didn't think I could muster the emotional energy to go through and sort those items, yet I kept moving the box to different locations around my house. Every time I looked at that box (sometimes a few times in a single day) I felt a pit in my stomach and thought, "I really need to go through that box." So the amount of mental, psychic and emotional energy that I didn't think I could manage in the few hours it took to sort that stuff leaked out slowly everyday for months! What a relief it was to just actually *deal with it.* All of my clients report that they feel energized and uplifted after they've done a major purge. They also become more sensitive to others trying to muck up their space (more on that later).

Everyone has different relationships with their stuff. Some people are more sentimental than others. But it is critical to take an honest look at our relationships with our belongings and the cost of living with these things. Disorganization and accumulation is a huge energy drain. As women are in the process of cleaning their 'hearth' (their environments), I would ask them the following questions: Are there things in my environment that I have accumulated mindlessly for no purpose? Do the things that surround me reflect who I am now and who I see myself becoming? I would recommend setting time aside for a purging and starting with one room at a time. Spiritually, I would suggest starting with the bedroom where you sleep and rest as the first space to clear. Another important space would be your creative work space as a good next step. If you live with others and have shared spaces, this will be a point of negotiation. I would NOT keep anything broken (get it repaired or get rid of it), anything useless, anything that makes you *feel bad,* or anything you have not used in over a year. Donate these things and put them *back into the universe* where someone else can use them. Do not "donate" this stuff to your friends or family *unless they actually, truly WANT* and need these items.

When my mother was alive and she was moving from her home to assisted living, we went through the purging process together. She had difficulty parting with a lot of things and it became a joke between my sister and me. We'd ask her "Do you want or need this?" And she'd say "No, but do *you* want it?" We felt a bad for her that we didn't want her unwanted stuff either. Be careful of not allowing yourself to be guilted into taking on other people's stuff just because they have difficulty letting go and they think giving it to you is better. I've had to learn over the years not to feel guilty about saying "no" to these 'gifts.' I've had family members get mad at me over this; actually one family member once said, "Beggars can't be choosers," and I replied, "I am NOT a beggar, and I *am* a chooser. Find someone else to take your unwanted things."

There are a number of really good books and videos specializing in decluttering your space (see recommended reading) so here I am just reviewing *why* this is so important from the standpoint of spiritual growth, transformation and change.

As you clear your physical items from your space, organize and become clear on your priorities, it is important to look holistically at all areas of your life and clean up your loose ends. Where are you sloppy and inattentive to your responsibilities? Is your life clogged with unnecessary tasks you've agreed to take on that really belong to others? Do you have the time and space to accomplish the things that are important to you in your day? Do you direct your life every day or is is dictated by others? I encourage my clients to listen to their bodies on this issue. Pay attention to feelings of annoyance, resentment or anger. These emotions can often be gifts that communicate that we've taken on things or responsibilities that are *not ours* to take on--to be blunt, *other people's shit.* It is important that we don't rescue our colleagues, friends and family members when their failure to plan or manage their lives becomes a crisis. When we swoop in and 'fix' things we take away the learning opportunity and chance to manage the major tasks of adult life: managing time, money, emotion and energy.

Start with sparks

Once we have our energy back (fuel), and we've cleaned our hearth (taken care of our shit), we can begin the process of re-sparking our creative flames. When our fires are burnt out or cold, it helps to start small to get our hearth restarted. It might feel hopeless and pointless (a main symptom of depression), and we can get easily discouraged and overwhelmed. To find a spark, you can try to revisit something you used to put creative energy into and try to bring this energy back, slowly. Some women find this brings up so much sadness and grief over the "lost" part of themselves that it is too painful to begin. If that is the case, try to spark with something new and small. Experiment with creating a meal you've never made before, decorate something, draw something, write a poem, put together an outfit that is really different from your usual style, make up a song--anything that puts you into a right-brain creative state. The outcome isn't important; the important thing is the creative energy you summon. Allowing time to journal and imagine are also important pursuits to re-spark passion and desire.

Fear of fire

Once we are ready to ignite our fires, we need to address the anxiety and fear that we might feel about our creative fires. It helps to think back to times when we were "too much" or *extra* (as my daughter likes to say). What happened when we were fully in our passion and power? Were we shunned? We were shamed into making ourselves small again? These are very real memories and fears for us to consider. To step into our power and passion, we need to deal with these memories and fears as they arise. Our brain is designed to keep us safe and avoid painful experiences. The process of growth, however, necessitates that we push through our brain's fear response and *feel the fear and do it anyway*. This is necessary for rewiring our brains and learning that we can be fully who we are as grown adult women, as chatelaines, and keep ourselves safe. The key is to start small, push ourselves just under the threshold of what we can tolerate and stay with our anxiety and fears until they naturally subside (when nothing actually bad happens). The nature of fear and anxiety is that it is *anticipatory*, meaning that it is most intense *before* the actual danger is upon us. The fear and anxiety, if one is able to stay with it, naturally subsides within a few minutes. Another key that is often used in therapy is the "worst case scenario." I will often have clients journal on the worst thing they can imagine and then also on *how* they might deal with that should it actually happen.

Air and space

Fire needs oxygen and space to burn. We are the only ones who know how much air and how much space (and time) we need to nurture and tend to our own creative fires. Some creative activities (like for me cooking or making things) are dynamic and fun both with noise and other people. Other creative endeavors are solitary pursuits. Many creative women I work with have a high need for space and quality (versus quantity) connection. Writing for me, for example, requires quiet, solitude and large chunks of uninterrupted time and space. A partner that does not support your creative pursuits, passions and fire is participating in *soul-killing*. They don't have to *like* the same things that inspire you, participate or even understand your passions, but they *do* need to give you the time and space to allow the kindling and burning of your fires. Keeping fire and passion in your life keeps you energized, youthful and interesting. You have the *right* to a life of energy and creativity. Often the people in our lives are fearful that we might leave them, outgrow them or lose interest in them. We can assure them that by allowing us time and space and a more balanced, energized life, we are better mothers, daughters, friends and lovers.

Good friends and allies can assist us in tending to our creative fires. Through support, interest or sometimes just holding us accountable to keeping our own fires going, they blow wind on our fires and keep them "stoked." The journal prompts below are designed to assist you with assessing the state of your creative fires.

Journal Prompts

Assessing your energy:

1. Do you have enough energy to do all that is important to you?

2. Do you have a process or routine for self-care?

3. Do you get enough rest and opportunity to refuel?

4. If you answered "no" to any of these questions, what needs to change and shift in your life right now? What is a plan or commitment you can make to yourself to rebalance your life? (*Be specific*)

Clearing your hearth:

1. What desires or dreams from the past are in ashes now?

2. Is it time to release these ashes in the wind or to re-spark that flame?

3. Do you accomplish all that is important to you in a day? A week? A month?

4. Is your home in order? Your desk/workspace? Your closets? Your bedroom?

5. Do you manage the business of your life? Do you meet your commitments? Are your bills paid on time?

6. Do you have stuff/activities/tasks in your life for no reason?

7. Does your life/environment reflect your vision for who you are and *who you see yourself becoming?*

8. Do you direct your life or is it dictated by others?

Carrying embers

1. What was the last thing you created?

2. What was the best thing you ever created?

3. Where is the passion in you alive at the moment?

4. What (or who) puts water on your fire?

The Victimhood Cage

This is a difficult cage to explore because women have often been victims of abuse and violence and presenting this as a "cage" is in no way suggesting that the victimization and pain are not real or that women are in any way responsible for the bad things that have happened to them. Quality therapy with a skilled and trusted professional is an important investment that needs to be attended to to heal the aftermath of abuse or violence, especially if you are stuck in a (bottom up-biological/neurological) trauma-fear response that prevents you from living in expansive and joyful ways. This chapter refers to *staying* in victimhood in our mental narratives as a form of disempowerment and ultimately a cage that keeps us trapped. Women sometimes confuse being a victim with victimhood. Victimhood is the single most disempowering stance that a woman can take from both a spiritual and a psychological perspective. How do we know when we are in this cage? We can see this cage/pattern when our conversations, stories, journals and narratives are filled with "this person did *this* to me..." and "this happened to me" and we stay stuck in that story long after the processing and healing stage should have occurred. This is where commitment to journaling is so crucial. We can't deny these patterns when they come up over and over in our pages in black and white.

On a vacation trip to Costa Rica two years after my divorce, I became aware of how much I wrote about and talked about all the ways I was wronged throughout the 17-year marriage, separation and divorce. It was only seeing it over and over in my journal that I finally had the epiphany: "God, I am so sick of this story, it is so boring - I can't stand to think about it or tell it anymore."

From that point forward, I dedicated myself to being highly conscious of every time I had a thought or snippet of any part of the narrative. I gave an edict to my brain, my heart and soul: "I've learned what I needed to from this. I won't be in this situation again so we can let this go now. We don't need to have the pain on repeat."

Why does our brain continue to hold onto our victim stories? The simple answer is "to keep us safe." We are biologically hardwired to remember negative and painful events vividly and repetitively so that we are sure to avoid them in the future. Our brain is doing its job; however, the fear-center (the amygdala) is a primitive system and a good servant that doesn't realize when the danger has truly passed, nor the fact that we also have higher levels of consciousness that can use our feminine powers of intuition and attuned instinct to keep us safe.

When we journal and track our dreams and inner and outer narratives and stories, these are all ways of backtracking and stalking the predator. Once we loop both the predator and the part of our own psyche that colluded with them, we can access our profound and proper instincts. This is where the predators are identified and banished forever. We can move from victim status to alert, awake, sharp-eared, wily, shrewd, and wild creatures.

Self-forgiveness

One of the most difficult things for most women to identify with is our inner-predator. In the teachings of indigenous peoples, there is an *agreement* between predators and prey. The agreement is that the predator will target the weak or sick members of the herd and the prey will let go and submit. The spirit of the prey animal leaves (disassociates) from the body *before* impact so that the animal doesn't have to experience the horror of being killed and eaten. When doing regression or past-life work, most of us can easily access when we have been victims. The greater challenge is to face that we have been *both* victim *and perpetrator*. It is essential that we get in touch with our inner-perpetrator and inner-predator as well as standing and facing when we might have behaved in these roles in our current lives. As difficult as this is and as much resistance as this brings up, it is essential for spiritual wholeness, healing and evolution. When we are victimized or abused in ongoing relationships of any kind, the inner-predator is often colluding with the external predator. This is why women are often suicidal when leaving these relationships. The inner-predator that we are unaware of, is trying to complete the job. This sounds really odd to many women, but it is these unspoken, unacknowledged aspects of ourselves that keep us feeling guilty and on some level, accepting of the abuse. We will keep cycling into predator-prey relationships. I believe that we often repeat these cycles because we are trying to master the outcomes and at least have a different (more empowering) outcome than before.

Often the women I have worked with will struggle with forgiving themselves on their healing journey. Since self-forgiveness is so crucial to helping reclaim their power and revive their intuitive nature, this must be explored. I hear: "How could I have allowed this to happen?", "How could I, as an intuitive woman, not have seen the true nature of this person or the situation?" These questions can also be framed with degrees of self-loathing, such as: "How could I have been so stupid?" Assisting a woman with understanding her own tendency to project onto others her own loving or good nature helps her to see that: 1) her victimization is absolutely not her fault consciously, 2) her unconscious may have colluded with the situation to try and master the dynamic and outcome and 3) her projections are a reflection of *what is good* in her nature, not a statement of blindness or stupidity. Again, I find that breaking down people as possessing an "S" self and an "s" self (see the previous chapter) helps us gain perspective.

We can fall in love with someone's "S" self, not realizing how much the "s" narcissistic and unevolved ego is driving the person's behavior. This can facilitate both forgiveness of both ourselves and the person who wronged us.

And on Rage

Once a woman acknowledges and begins to process her victimizations, she experiences rage. This is rightful rage. I describe to my clients that emotions are like the keys on a piano. Deep grief and despair are the lowest notes on the keyboard with joy and ecstacy at the highest notes. Rage is an octave up from deep grief and moving vibrationally-speaking in the higher direction. Culturally and socially, most women have great difficulty experiencing, expressing and processing rage. It is one of the emotions that are forbidden in families and in the larger culture. She either needs to learn to express it incrementally in ways that are not destructive to herself and others or the energy implodes and she turns this inward on herself. The suppression of rage is exhausting and a huge energy and power drain. Acknowledging and dissipating the energies trapped within the rage is freeing and part of power reclamation. Physical expression through activities like kick-boxing, running or other vigorous expressions of the body can be helpful. Vocal expressions such as yelling at the top of her lungs or singing loudly to angry songs/lyrics can assist. I once had a client take a plastic bat to a pile of sandbags. Tearing up items or throwing them can also release pent-up energies. The most important part of release work though, is the acknowledgment that the rage is there and it is justified, but that now it is time to be released, to free up that energy and move forward.

In addition to releasing pent-up anger and rage, the inner-predator in a woman's psyche must be dismembered and dealt with as well. In many ancient stories, the predator is dismembered and carried away by ravens, raptors or vultures. That energy is digested and transmuted to a form that is energy but no longer destructive. As in other aspects of truth-seeing and telling we must be willing to face and acknowledge all the parts of ourselves, even those we find reprehensible. This allows us to be more balanced and conscious of those energies and aspects operating in our lives. Predators have an important place in the ecosystem, but it can be disastrous if this gets out of balance.

Self-acceptance

A final aspect of releasing victimhood is in self-acceptance. We reclaim our power in realizing that we have survived what might have destroyed us. Over time and by acknowledging and integrating *all* aspects of our stories we become heroines of our own life. Letting go of guilt and shame is a way of honoring ourselves and putting our stories in proper perspective. Often it is in the telling or writing of our stories and getting confirmation, feedback or the witness of our sisters that we can truly see our stories in a new and more healing light. A writing assignment I often give to my clients is to write their stories while focusing on the phrases, "I made this choice and this happened... I made this decision and this happened..." as well as focusing on the strengths, resilience, learning and post-traumatic growth points in their story.

Journal Prompts

1. Spend time paying close attention to the stories you tell yourself and others on a habitual basis and look for clues that this may be a 'victimhood' story that needs revision. Rewrite the story by a) taking responsibility for your choices, actions and role within it and b) focusing on the strengths gained or lessons learned.

2. Move from asking the question, "Why did this happen?" to asking, "What did I learn? What strengths did I find that I didn't know I had? What did I gain from this experience?"

3. What is the doorway that the predator enters? Where am I seducible? Thinking back, did I have instinctual messages of any kind that I may have ignored?

The
Keys

The Keys: Intuition & Intention
Your Most Powerful Gifts

Intuition is the first and most important key for transformation and deeply connected and necessary for the other keys as well. I am defining intuition as the internal wisdom and guidance system that is your birthright. While some women have more developed skills at accessing and trusting their intuition, *everyone* has this gift, this system and access to their intuitive abilities. Regardless of circumstances or the cage you are in at the moment, accessing, developing and trusting your intuition is the key to your path and journey forward now and for the rest of your life. First I want to discuss what intuition *is,* as well as what it is *not.*

Intuition is receiving the messages from the divine source, directing us to our eternal nature and light and our soul's creative expression in our lifetime. Intuition is loving, gentle and powerful. It does not flatter the ego, but instead supports your soul's true essence (the capital "S" self). Developing intuition is joyful work- not painful work and there can be many channels, or paths to the way that information comes to you. For some women, intuition comes as hearing a still, small voice, for others it is visual sign, for some it comes in body sensations or in our dream state. Learning to access your soul's intuition benefits not only your own life immensely, but also those around you and the larger world of humanity. The energy of your development and personal evolution provides impulse and momentum for the spiritual evolution of the larger human collective. In other words, when you do your individual spiritual work, you are healing your ancestral line as well as helping *everyone* in the conscious collective.

The aspects you must overcome on the path to grasp the key of intuition are fear, issues of self-worth and sometimes, religious-training blocks. Once you have successfully navigated these, then it is a matter of practice, practice, practice so that you trust your own inner guidance and then continue fine tuning it as you travel your life's path.

Fear of your intuitive gifts

The women I work with have often been socially conditioned by their families or religion to fear their gifts. Often, there is a faulty perspective that somehow the intuition about something has *caused* this situation and women are afraid that accessing their gifts might *cause* something bad to happen. Sometimes they fear intuition because they are afraid of seeing something painful or unpleasant. My perspectives on this are that women who are in their power and trusting their intuition are a threat to the patriarchal power structures because we can not be controlled. We need to take heed of individuals or institutions that would seek to stifle the gifts of our spiritual power. Life involves painful or difficult circumstances and intuition merely gives us a 'heads-up' about these events or protects us from them.

One of the important things to learn about intuition is that most of the time, it is not driven by fear itself, rather it is a still, small, loving sense or voice within us. Intuition might fly in the face of the rational or logic, however, it is not coercive, nor would it violate our most sacred values. To access this without all the excess noise and emotion, we need to find the time and space to quiet our minds. Intuition comes to us when we are in receptivity.

The self-worth ("s") block

Here is that issue again! Self-worth is another obstacle many women face in believing that they are not worthy of spiritual power, gifts and intuition. Again, organized religions have really done a great job of persecuting and suppressing spiritual women throughout the last several centuries. Women carry a collective deep soul-wound in our psyches from this history. It is no wonder many of us are afraid to assert our spiritual gifts and power. Religions that focus on women as inherently sinful often use shame as a mechanism for ultimate spiritual control. I like to remind my daughter and her peers that we are the great-granddaughters of the witches they could not burn.

Related to the issue of self-worth is the abdication of our spiritual power. We give up our power for love, for belonging, to avoid conflict and because we are afraid. We tell ourselves that others (authorities) know better. This means we give up our inner-knowing or power before it has had an opportunity to take root and grow. I would argue that no one knows your soul ("S" self) and purpose more than you, even when you are very young. Fortunately I learned this lesson very early on, at around age three.

When I was around three years old, we took a family trip to visit some friends of my parents. They were in a rural area with a large back yard. From the time we arrived and got out of the car I was uneasy and afraid to go on the property. I was particularly afraid of the family dog, a Dalmatian. This was unusual for me as I have loved and not had a fear of animals for my entire life. The host family and my parents were insistent that this dog was loving and friendly. I would not go into the back yard until the dog was on a lead. Their little girl who was around my age ran up to the dog and hugged it around the neck to prove it was a nice dog. They made me go up to him and pet the top of its head. The dog jumped up, knocked me down and bit me in the face. I still have a tiny scar from one of his teeth by my left eye. It has reminded me throughout my life to trust my intuition over adults or those more powerful than me. My parents told me later the dog had been diagnosed with distemper and had to be put down.

The pathways of intuitive guidance

You can expect that intuition may come into your awareness in a variety of ways. Somatic (body sensations) experiences, such as a feeling in the throat, chest or gut or tingling sensations or goosebumps are ways intuition might enter through the body senses. Clairaudience or hearing a small voice, clairvoyance or visual sensations, telepathy or precognition either waking or in dreams are all ways in which our intuitive impulses come to us. You need to 1) be open to intuitive messages, 2) expect that you will receive guidance, 3) trust the guidance and 4) act on the guidance you receive.

Getting started

Accessing intuition requires a relaxed and receptive mind and body. It doesn't take much time (10 to 15 minutes a day) but the important thing is doing this regularly. I like to have this as a part of my morning routine as it helps me get into the right mindset for my day. If I am seeing clients, I incorporate asking for guidance for my work with the day's clients as well. I always record my experiences in a journal and writing everything counts. Sometimes it is only looking back at my entries that I realize the significance of a particular message or experience. If mornings are too hectic for you, choose another time to do this - for example, on your lunch break, or at the end of the day if you are not too tired to focus.

Many women have the false idea that mediation has to be difficult or complicated. It isn't. Quite simply, meditation is the art of relaxing your body, quieting your mind and learning to hold your attention and focus on one thing. For most people the easiest way to this state is focusing on the breath and taking slow deep deliberate breaths. All that it takes is breathing for a count of 4, holding for 4 and then exhaling;

do this several times over and slowly allow your awareness to expand into the room. I have developed the practice of imagining a door where my heart center is opening slowly until it is wide open. Some women find sitting still to be very difficult and, if that is the case, you can do "active" forms of meditation while you are moving or doing something else, provided that you can get into the open, relaxed, receptive state where your mind is calm. Over time and with practice you'll develop your own routines.

Tools for aaccessing intuition

Tools can be enormously helpful to accessing intuition. Burning sage or other plants, candles or essential oils can assist us in getting into a 'prayerful' state of mind. The major religious practices around the world use candles, incense or herbs as tools for helping access prayerful states of mind. Tools send a message to our minds and bodies that we are doing something special and outside our ordinary consciousness. Music, chanting or singing can also assist with transforming our mental state by changing our vibrations and our brainwaves and is also used by the majority of the world's spiritual traditions. Music from the Baroque era has shown evidence of assisting people with achieving the brainwaves associated with meditative states.

Using a journal as a part of the practice and doing automatic writing can also be powerful. This form of journal sends a message to your unconscious mind to release messages and guidance from your higher states of consciousness.

Using writing to access intuition

Getting into a relaxed and prayerful state and writing without censure is an excellent active way to hone and practice accessing intuition. Most of my clients start first with inspirational writing and then move on to a more formal automatic writing if they find this pathway is a powerful fit for them. I would define inspirational writing as writing a letter to one's soul or higher-wisdom self, ("S" self) spiritual guides or even loved ones who have passed on. In this letter, one asks for guidance to solve a particular problem or make an important decision. The responses that are 'imagined' are typically divinely inspired and a bit different than our ordinary writing language or style. Automatic writing is a little more advanced in that it requires even more surrender of the mind, intellect and ego. It is called 'automatic' because the thinking is that we are allowing our spirit to borrow our hand and write the responses. This type of intuition access typically requires lots of practice.

Other tools that I have found helpful when teaching clients to access intuition are the use of cards or books. Jung and a number of archetypal psychologists who've followed him have written on the use of divination, specifically the Tarot, as a means for accessing the collective unconscious and inspiration[10]. Choosing a reading deck (Tarot cards, for example) is highly personal and I'd suggest seeing which symbols and images you are drawn to at this time in your journey. Since I have been using these tools for decades, I have collected many decks over the years, including Soulful Women cards, Horse cards, Bird cards and several Tarot decks. Pulling a daily card with a message and recording it and seeing how that message plays itself out in your day, or even using an inspirational book and turning to random pages as guidance is helpful in developing a practice. I do more complicated readings/card pulls when I need symbolic clarity on a challenging time or situation.

A few of my tools...

10. For reading on Jung and the Tarot see Fink, J. K. (2022). Archetypal Tarot: The Art of Seeing Through. *Jung Journal, 16*(2), 62-74.

Developing trust

When you have set an intention to access and use your intuition *always,* you begin to develop a trust of it, a deep inner-knowing. This starts on the small stuff and builds over time. If you don't develop a sense of trust over relatively low-stakes issues, you will find it very very difficult to trust your intuition on bigger issues when stakes and emotions are high. When you are trying to use intuition on emotionally charged or complex questions or issues - this is typically when the ego butts in. One of my early mentors and teachers used to encourage making intuition an "I wonder" game throughout your day. For example, I wonder who is calling? I wonder what is the best way to drive to work? I wonder who I am going to run into today?...This is where journaling is so important. You can look at all the examples on your journey of when you accessed, valued and acted on your intuition and the results. This helps build a track record of confidence that can not be underestimated.

Fine-tuning your intuitive gifts

I define fine-tuning as developing a moment-by-moment awareness of intuitive messages during the course of your day and daily (non-meditative) activities. This includes but is not limited to reading the energies of others and accessing wisdom of knowledge not accessible by ordinary states of conscious awareness. For some of you, this may evolve into accessing intuition and reading for others. One of the biggest issues with fine-tuning is that we live in a bubble. We filter everything we see, hear and notice through our constructed 'lens' and call it reality. We tend to rearrange and reconstruct the 'truth' so that it fits our world. We live in the myth that there is an objective reality or truth when in fact, everything is *subjective*. When we are trying to hone and strengthen (fine-tune) our intuition, we need to practice expanding our awareness and paying close attention to details without modifying them to fit our narrow lens. We can increase our ability to pay attention to details by making a practice of 'noticing' (not judging, mind you, just noticing). Noticing as many details in your environment as possible, noticing as many details as you can in your interactions with people throughout your day, noticing every word you can in a conversation. This requires present moment awareness and turning down the constant mind-chatter in our heads. Additionally, noticing what is going on inside you, in your own energy and body as you move throughout your day, is essential. For example, *how do I feel in my body right now during this interaction? Does my encounter with this person energize me or drain me? Where am I involuntarily constricting my muscles? Where do I lose focus? Where does my mind wander? What am I doing with my breathing? If you ask for confirmation you will always receive it.*

More than 20 years ago, I had an encounter with an individual in which my intuition saved my life. I was attending a two-day conference in the city and commuted by train. I took a seat in the auditorium and started chatting with the man sitting next to me. His name tag indicated that he was from the town next to mine. He seemed friendly enough and I causally mentioned, "We could have ridden the train together." As the weekend went on, I became increasingly uncomfortable with him being next to me. He started insisting that I take a ride home from him at the end of the conference rather than taking the train. My husband at the time would have delighted at this since he was majorly annoyed and inconvenienced at having to drive me. At a break in the conference I headed to the ladies room, carrying a large stack of books that I purchased. He tried to insist that I leave my books with him, which I refused, and he got inappropriately angry. I was young and questioning why this was feeling so off to me and why I had such powerful negative feelings (instincts). I went into the stall and prayed and quieted my mind.

"Spirit, please send a message about this so I know what to do," and clearly and as loud as if there was someone in there with me, I heard: "If you go with him, you will never see your family again." I had a powerful, undeniable, sick feeling in my gut at that moment.

Now I was uncomfortable about even walking all the way to the train station so I called my husband at the time and demanded he pick me up, which he did begrudgingly. While I was waiting for him to get pick me up, this guy insisted on waiting with me at the front of the conference center. I stayed where there were lots of people around. I said, "I don't need you to wait for me...I'm a big girl," to which he said (unbelievably), "There are lots of big girls out there and things happen to them." He waited until he saw me get in the car with my husband and infant son. I don't know what might have befallen me had I not been intuitive and also checking-in with and trusting my instincts and intuition, but it was a powerful lesson I have never forgotten.

Journal Prompts on Intuition

1). Think back on your life and detail all the times you were guided by your intuition. Note a) how or with what senses the intuition came to you (hearing? body sensation? visual?), b) how did you act on the intuition (or not?) c) what was the outcome?

2). How do you get into a relaxed and receptive state of mind? What interferes with this?

3). Choose a physical tool to help you access intuition through symbols... detail a) why you are drawn to this particular tool at the present time and b) record your daily experiences in working with this tool.

Intention

Intention is the second key that is essential in living a life of freedom as the chatelaine in your life. This is intentionally *after* the section on intuition. This is because accessing and trusting your intuition is the way to let the power of intention flow through. Intention is a powerful, clear focus on what you desire without a rationale and without justification. It just *is*. This is where your power is and where it is activated. Intention provides the direction for our creative and spiritual energies and is at the heart of the other keys as well. It refers to not only our behavior, what we *intend* to do, it also refers to what we want to *bring about.*

Intention is when the heart, mind and will are all simultaneously engaged in moving towards a desire. I like to use the example of young children here. If you have ever had a three-year-old who is really focused on something that they want, they have their heart, mind and will all engaged at the same time and they are a force to be reckoned with! It is *very* difficult to thwart their desires. In his book *The Power of Intention*, Dr. Wayne W. Dyer describes how someone living in the field of intention is very much like this in that no matter how other people try to dissuade them and give them all the reasons that they might fail, they are undeterred.

Anything that exists in the material world began as an idea in the imagination. The chair I am sitting on right now and the laptop I am writing on first begin in the minds of those who created it. The creators *intended* these items into being. So too are *all* the aspects of your life. In order to create and move into the life you are envisioning for yourself, you must first trust your inner guidance system of intuition and, second, establish your sacred intentions.

Getting Clear and Writing your Intentions

We are always manifesting and creating our worlds. What most people don't recognize is that we are often unintentionally doing this in a very sloppy manner. Since we create what we focus on, if we continually focus on what is not working, what is missing and the obstacles we face, we continually get more of the same. When we keep focusing on the cages we are in rather than imagining our near-future selves outside of the cage, we stay stuck. We often are stuck because we keep asking why questions. "Why is this happening to me?" Or "why is this person behaving this way?" Rather than the more power *how* questions such as "how can I find a creative solution to this?" How can I learn and grown from this situation?" or, "How can I transform my experience of this?"

Many of the women I work with say they do not know what they want. I think this is *partially* true. I believe that too often they have been conditioned to repress or bury their deepest desires. Even as young girls, they may have been *thwarted*, shamed or punished in the expression of desires. As a result, they coped by burying their sacred dreams and desires so deeply inside them they didn't have to endure the pain of despair and longing. For women who are not clear on what they want, we start slowly with one particular aspect of life that they want to transform and go from there.

Intentions are not only made by getting clear in your heart and mind; I believe that writing them is also important to the manifestation. I am sure my clients get really tired of me insisting that they use a journal but I do this because I *know* that in the mind, brain, spirit and soul, there is power that comes from the act of writing that I have not found an alternative or replacement for. There is an art to this and there are a number of good books and sources on this (provided in the recommended reading) for more detailed work. Basically, the intentions need to be written in the present tense, affirmative and also with emotion (heart). For example, "I am loving my _____" or "I am enjoying _____" or "I am so grateful for _____."

Intention also needs to be paired with aligned and intuition-inspired action. You need to be willing to act on your impulses and inner-guidance. You need to prepare and pave the way for your manifestations to come as well. It is important that everything is in alignment. For example, if I have an intention of something I really want in my life, but many of my actions or resources are flowing in the opposite way and are actually taking me further away, I am not in alignment.

I have loved sharing this concept with my daughter with the hopes that she too will learn this by my example. When we found our horse property in late fall of 2020, I showed her my journal entry from 2014 in which I wrote all of the intentions I had for a horse property. There it is in black and white, undeniably *all* of the qualities and aspects of our place, with only one exception. I had written the names of towns with horse properties with trains to the city where I worked and the phrase "a train to the city 20 minutes away". Even though I am in a totally different state than I thought I'd be living in, there are not one but two train stations within 20 minutes of me. It took a few years to arrive, and we went through many difficult transitions and changes before we landed here, but I love where I am living and it is even better than what I intended and what I imagined in 2014.

Paris, Paris and Paris

When I was a little girl I wrote down in my diary that I wanted to live in Paris. For whatever reason I was obsessed with Paris and all things French including the language. As the years went on I forgot about this desire. In 2018, after a difficult period around my birthday, I wrote in my journal *"Next year I will spend my birthday in Paris,"* not knowing how in the world that might happen. Many months later I was chosen to go to France on a Vincentian Heritage Trip with my university and when I looked at the itinerary, I couldn't believe it. We had a free-day to ourselves *in Paris* on my birthday. In our horse Sugar's papers her dam was named *Paris* and when a woman bought one of our ponies, RB she changed his name to Paris! When we celebrated my first birthday here on the farm, I realized that our farm is in the township of Paris!

Paris, France (2019)   Paris Farm (2021)

Dealing with resistance and doubt

When working with intentions, it is really important to be honest with the doubts, thoughts and feelings that arise. If there are conflicts or resistance, you need to address these and soothe them so you can be open to the outcome and the guidance toward your intentions. Many times our doubts and resistance are old woundings, old beliefs or patterns from the past that we really need to clear and get rid of. I tell my clients that beliefs are nothing more than something you have thought so much that it *feels true*. We can shift and change our beliefs. We can let go of beliefs that are not soul and life-affirming and beliefs that no longer serve us. Similar to the blocks we have in accessing and trusting our intuition, religious training blocks and issues of self-worth may be impeding the creation of the life we want.

Taking care of our seeds

As women, we have a 'leg-up' on the energy of intention as we already have activated within our bodies the energy of creative potential. This is true whether or not we have created biological children. The same creative energy potential can be used in every area of our lives. When a woman discovers she is pregnant, she often holds this knowledge to herself while she adjusts to this new state of being. In a protective way, she may also be selective in who she shares the news with during the stages of her pregnancy. We can also view giving birth to our intentions in this same way. In the early stages, our dreams and intentions are most fragile and our doubts and fears may be easily activated. It is really important that we protect our intentions and dreams in the early stages until they take root and can stand on their own. Our egos, our friends and families need "evidence" of manifestation of our dreams and intentions, and this often creates blocks for us. You need to know with whom you can share your deepest dreams and intentions.

Journal Prompts

Writing Intentions

1). **What is a dream or desire that you are longing for at this time?**

2). **Write it in the affirmative, present tense.** (For example, *Intention: To have a healthy romantic relationship--"* I am enjoying my new relationship with my romantic partner")

3). **When you write your intention(s) pay close attention to any conflicting thoughts or doubts that arise** (it is hard to meet quality romantic partners, there aren't any good potential partners, I have to go through a lot of effort, heartache or drama to find my partner"). Address each one of these as a belief you've picked up along your path, not a fact.

4). Commit to following intuition, guidance and any inspired-aligned action that will bring this intention closer.

🗝🗝🗝

The Keys:
Integrating Transition
Ritual and Ceremony

Human beings are ritualistic by nature and the practice and creation of ceremony and ritual is as old as time itself. Ritual builds a powerful bridge between our unconscious and conscious minds. Even as children, rituals, such as those at bedtime, help signal to the mind, body and spirit that the day is over and it is time for sleep. Rituals can be especially important to children in that they help children navigate a world in which they often have little agency and control. Rituals provide us with a sense of comfort, predictability and groundedness in our lives. These rituals are beyond mere routines in that they have emotional and psychological meaning and value to us. If my routine changes, when I am on vacation for example, I'm not too disrupted and in many ways this leaves me open to insights I would not normally have in my routine life.

Beyond mere routine, ritual has much greater significance in that we imbue it with meaning and *intention*. These practices become especially important in times of great stress and when life becomes chaotic, as they ground us back into our bodies, in present-moment-awareness and remind us of mindful intention. Anthropologists and social scientists have long argued over the definitions of ritual. Here, I define ritual as a very personal set of purposeful actions with intention. These can range from the simple (I sit and have my morning coffee in a certain chair while the sun comes up and start my day in a state of calm reflection and journaling) to the more complex (I create a ritual to mark the passing of a beloved pet). Ritual connects us with our metaphoric, imaginal mind and psyche in a powerful non-ordinary way. Since these are ancient practices, stored in our collective human consciousness, most people find them powerful and effective even if they are not religious. In my definition here, since ritual is *personal* it can be created or made up by anyone at any time the need arises. There is a deep psychological reason why we have held on to this practice throughout all of our human growth and evolution through deep time. High performance athletes have often revealed rituals or practices that they used to prepare them for peak performance (including the use of "lucky" items). Recently, psychological science has explored and found evidence supporting that ritual improves mood and functioning.[11]

Ceremony, on the other hand, I define as much more formal, proscribed and community-oriented. Also ancient, ceremonies have been part of all human cultures since the beginning of time. Ceremonies are created by cultures, subcultures, communities or families and passed down to future generations. There are sacred ceremonies that societies and cultures reserve the right to keep secret or only share with permission. Other ceremonies are more freely shared

---

11. Gino, F., & Michael, I. (2013). Norton."Why Rituals Work.". *Scientific American, 14.*

or adopted cross-culturally and evolve over time. Similar to ritual, but more complex, the function of ceremony is to assist with physical and psychological transition. Ceremonies fall into several categories: 1) stage of physical life-span ceremonies marking rites of passage--birth, adolescence, menarche, menopause and death, 2) social cohesion ceremonies, 3) ceremonies to mark the natural seasons and connect us to the natural world and 4) ceremonies that mark beginnings and endings.

I write about ritual and ceremony as keys because these are time-tested human practices that help us with change and transition. Many of the women I work with do this intuitively, they just don't necessarily recognize it consciously right away. For example, women often cut off their hair when they have gone through a major life transition such as getting married, having a baby or getting divorced. Every time she looks in the mirror she is reminded of her new state and new identity that she needs to integrate into her consciousness. The younger women in my practice put themselves through an 'initiation' ordeal and get tattoos or piercings to mark that they have been through something significant and are now walking differently in the world. Women will burn letters or pictures or items of their exes as a means for marking the death of the relationship (fire cremation is a very effective tool for transformation!). There are steps involved with every effective ceremony or ritual. The first step is *intention*. This section purposely follows the key of intention because that is the most important piece to any ceremony or ritual. All rituals have a beginning, a middle with a climax, an end and finally the task of integration of what happened in the ritual.

A personal ritual at the start of the pandemic (2020)

Rituals from my women's group

An October 31st ancestor altar honoring those who have passed on

Setting Sacred Intention:

This is the most important aspect of a ritual. What is the purpose of the ritual action? Is it to release something (or someone) from your life that no longer serves you? Is it to activate healing of a particular physical or soul issue? Are you trying to release or let go of a destructive pattern or bad habit? Are you focusing on a goal or desire such as prosperity? It is really important to have clarity on what the ritual should help you achieve. Additionally, in whose light are you doing this? What power or energy are you calling upon? In religious rituals, god is invoked, however, non-religious women can still call in the powers of nature or their ancestors for energy and assistance.

The Beginning: Leaving the Old Self or Past Behind.

The entry or start of the ritual should mark that you are entering non-ordinary sacred space. This can be created by marking a physical space, such as a circle or entryway, so we know we are entering to do something special. Preparing in advance by bathing or wearing certain clothes or items is helpful. Burning candles, sage or incense can also make the space sacred. Even in my therapy work, I view our sessions in a ritualistic way. Once the client comes through the door of the office (or the arena if I am working with my horses), we both know we are entering a sacred space. I use sage or the diffusion of essential oils to keep the space clear. We take our physical places and I typically say something like, "Let's arrive in the space," or "settle in" as a cue to relax and let the outside world and issues go for the time being and then we "check-in."

The Middle: Creating a Climax Where the Change Occurs.

In the middle of the ritual is where the symbolic change occurs and where there is an emotional climax or highpoint through physical action. For example, burning something or releasing something, cutting something. In most marriage ceremonies, the climax is the exchange of vows, rings and the sealing of the promises with a kiss. In baptism rites, it is the anointing of the head with oils or water. To revisit my 'therapy as ritual' example from above, the middle or climax might be the moment of insight a client has or when a healing moment (release of tears) or release occurs.

The End: Celebrating the 'New' State of Being.

The end of a ritual is critical: closing the sacred work is important and allowing ourselves to celebrate that we've done something special and that we are different on the other side of the ritual. I often give tokens such as beads, stones, feathers or pinecones[12] from the trees on my land for participants to take away to remind them of the commitments or energies that we invoked during our work.

It is really important to carry the energy of the ritual back into our ordinary consciousness and to integrate it into our lives. It is critical that our families, friends and communities also recognize our changes and new state of being. This is where rites of passage for adolescents really fall apart in modern Western culture. There is not a clear delineation of when an adolescent officially leaves childhood and becomes an adult. It it when they have sex for the first time? When they can legally vote or join the armed services? Or when they can legally drink

---

12. Pinecones are important ancient symbols of spiritual enlightenment in many cultures and represent the pineal gland in the brain.

alcohol? This is even more confusing for young men, because at least for young women menarche is a *clear* undeniable event that indicates the leaving behind of childhood and the start of adult womanhood.

Modern ritual for entering womanhood

When my daughter was 11, I held a ceremony to celebrate her entry into *Moontime* (womanhood). I created a ritual customized in collaboration with her and relevant for her as a modern young girl living in the urban Midwest. It is important to note that she was raised with these types of events and we had been talking about this since she was young. I gave her the option of inviting any of her girlfriends who may have gone through their transition already, but she chose to keep this private from her friends from school. I worked with her on the planning to make sure she was comfortable with the plan and not embarrassed about any of it as that would have completely defeated the purpose of the ritual. This was *not* about me or what I wanted, it was about her. I was just experienced at facilitating such things and wanted to work *with her* on what would feel special and positive.

Twenty-six women, all close friends and family, gathered for this in my small living room. Our *intention* was to mark her entry into this new biological and psychological phase of her life in a way that was much more spiritual and healthier than whatever messages she might receive from the dominant

American culture. In preparation, we smudged all the women and called in all of the spirits of our grandmothers and great-grandmothers.

For the *middle* of the ceremony or *climax*, we had a wide satin white ribbon that had been a tied around my daughter's waist at the start of the ceremony to signify her girlhood. At the middle, each woman gave her words of advice or wisdom about being a young woman as they tied new thin red ribbons (signifying entry into *maiden*hood) on her wrists. After she made it all the way around to each woman in the circle, I cut the white ribbon on her waist. I gifted her with red ruby ring to wear on her lefthand ring finger.

For the *ending* and celebration we had a crescent moon-shaped cake and a moon-themed party. The women who came brought gifts of self-care, beauty and hair accessories (not pads or tampons, *please).* While I can say this was powerful for my daughter, she had grown up with *me* as her mother, so I think it was normal for her. I had written a short manuscript called "Luna's Daughters: Welcoming Our Daughters to Womanhood" for my senior thesis project as an undergraduate student at DePaul well before she was born, so I had been preparing her for years. I think for her two grandmothers, my mother and my mother-in-law, it was profound and healing. I was a little worried they would handle this like, "What *crazy* thing is Arieahn doing now?" But that is not what happened. They were moved to tears and recounted their own experiences with their first menstruation (which, with no surprise, were largely shame-filled and negative). Both grandmothers kept saying how they wished they had something like this. Most of the women who came also found this celebration affirming. More than a decade later, these women remind me of this ceremony occasionally. My words to Ciara that day were, "Take a look around this room at all these women gathered here. My prayer and wish for you is that someday you are fortunate enough to have such a wonderful group of women surrounding you." Again, healing in a moment, traveling up and down the generations through time.

There are a number of good books and resources both in print and online for creating rituals. An older source that I really love is Adele Getty's *A Sense of the Sacred*. My most recent work in ritual for various groups has focused on healing divisions and letting go of grief caused by both the pandemic and the cultural and racial wounds that have come to the surface to be addressed and healed. In the final section, *Being a Chatelaine*, I offer a few daily ritual suggestions as well.

Journal Prompts on Ritual and Ceremony

1. What issue or transition would you like to address in a ritual?

2. Using your creativity and intuition, what tools or actions might you use for your ritual?

3. Do you need to do this alone or with others?

4. What would be the perfect timing and space for this?

5. How will the ritual begin? What will happen in the middle? The end? How will you celebrate or integrate the change you are focused on?

The Keys:
Body-wisdom, Sex and Power

The single most powerful weapon to disarm
and disempower a woman is SHAME.

Women have always been closely aligned with nature by virtue of our fecundity; this has persisted throughout the world's cultures, languages and history. The fate of women and of the natural world has always been intimately intertwined. Many of the world's philosophic and religious traditions have encouraged a separation of the mind and body as a higher state of being. However, for women this is impossible and a disaster. Prior to the 16th century, the view of the earth and nature was "an organic cosmos with a living female earth at its center".[13] As philosophies have devalued the natural world and aspired to 'rise above' it, women and nature have both suffered. The connection between women, nature and the 'fall' of man from the Garden of Eden proposed by 17th century philosopher Francis Bacon and those who succeeded him, still pulses under our modern narratives. Bacon, who was Lord Chancellor to King James and was commissioned to write the King James version of the Bible, was a prolific author and highly influential thinker. Bacon asserted that man had lost his rightful dominion over nature and animals

---

13. Merchant, C. (1980). The death of nature: Women, ecology, and the scientific revolution. Preface

as a result of the Fall caused by Eve. The principal villain in Bacon's narrative of recovery of man's dominion was both women and nature herself.[14] I mention this here because there is such a long history of misunderstanding, domination, and abuse of the feminine in our social and cultural constructions. These concepts are so central to religion, culture and even medicine, that women (and men) don't recognize these as *just ideas* (not facts) or understand the ways in which this impacts our beliefs and experiences of ourselves, our bodies, our power and our sexuality. Getting in touch with our body-wisdom and learning to love and accept our bodies and our sexuality is a key to our energy and power.

How did it go wrong?

It is essential that we recognize the inherent power in our bodies and in our sexuality. There is a reason why rape, sexual abuse and shaming are used as weapons against women. These experiences can effectively cut us off from our true natures, our intuition, our orgasmic creative energy and our power. Of all of these, shame seems to have the longest, lasting effect. I find it interesting that many of the patriarchal religions of the world focus on shame as a means for ultimate control. I also find it interesting that powerful women in history have been accused of being sexually inappropriate as attempts to bring them to heel. To return to the Garden of Eden theme, I love the metaphor of the garden in the book *Come As You*

---

14. Excellent resource on this topic is Merchant, C. (2004). *Reinventing Eden: The fate of nature in Western culture*. Routledge

Are by sex-educator Emily Nagoski, in which she describes women's sexuality as a garden:

"On the day you were born, you're given a little plot of rich and fertile soil, slightly different from everyone else. And right away your family and your culture start to plant things and tend the garden for you until you are old enough to take over its care yourself. They plant language and attitudes and knowledge about love and safety and bodies and sex... you didn't choose any of that."[15]

She goes on to describe that, as we reach adolescence and begin to tend our gardens on our own, we may find that our families and cultures may have planted beautiful, healthy things and you may have noticed things you want to change. Some women are lucky with what gets planted, and some of us get stuck with toxic crap in our garden and we are stuck with the tasks of uprooting all the junk and replacing it with something better and healthier that we choose for ourselves.

We live in a crazy culture

I was born in the early 1960s during the 'sexual revolution' and the second wave of women's liberation (the first wave in the U.S. was in the mid- to late 1800s). The widespread availability

15. Nagoski, E. (2015). *Come as you are: The surprising new science that will transform your sex life.* Simon and Schuster., p. 45

of birth control pills coincided with women entering the workforce demanding equal pay for equal work. Six decades later, we are *still* struggling for equality and our reproductive rights are again in question and under threat from patriarchal, oppressive powers. Our culture is notorious in sending mixed messages about women's sexuality and power, so what we achieve with advances in legislation and reproductive rights is often mitigated or even undone by conflicting messages from our media and culture. Women are expected to be objects of desire, yet remain pure. Powerful women are criticized if they don't meet certain standards of beautify and desirability, yet if a woman is desirable and powerful, she is often accused of using her sexuality in manipulative ways. Telling a man he is not masculine is way of shaming him, telling a woman she is a slut is how culture shames her. For men it is a source of pride to having many sexual conquests, for women it is a source of shame. From society's point of view, men are designed to desire sex and women are designed to withhold it. Science and research has indicated, however, that there are very few gender differences in desire. Women, though, are raised and socialized to *not* express it. Since there is such an energetic, spiritual and psychological link between sex and power, it is presented as a key.

As a part of this key, it is also essential that we recognize and resist the over-sexualization or objectification of our young daughters in ways that cause harm. In 2007, the APA Task Force on the Sexualization of Girls published research on the content and effects of virtually every form of media aimed at girls and young women.[16] Sexualization was defined by researchers as occurring when a person's value comes only from sexual appeal or behavior to the exclusion of other characteristics, and when a person is sexually objectified or made into a *thing* for another's sexual use.

Researchers found that sexualized media that presented girls and women as sexual *objects* had a number of negative consequences to the mental health of girls including cognitive functioning, physical and mental health problems, body image issues and sexual development. The media's emphasis on sexualization and objectification of girls had negative effects on girls' confidence and comfort in their own bodies and increased shame and anxiety. Other mental health issues such as eating disorders, low self-esteem, depression and the inability to develop a healthy sexual self-image were all indicated as effects of sexualization. The report called on parents, schools and mental health professionals to be alert for the potential impact on girls and young women. This study was conducted more than a decade ago, and I suspect that the proliferation of social media and the constant comparison to images that may or may not be real has now made the problems even more widespread. As women, we can combat these negative impacts by healing our own issues and histories with our sexuality and then, by teaching our daughters what health sexuality *is,* as well as what it is *not.* Women often make the mistake of trying to bolster their daughters sense of identity and confidence by focusing on all the other attributes

16. American Psychological Association. (2008). Report of the APA Task Force on the Sexualization of Girls.

they possess while ignoring sexuality. If we do this, we leave our daughters vulnerable to having those *cancelled out* in her psyche during adolescence by the power of negative sexuality before she has enough knowledge and sophistication to shield herself.

Discovering or rediscovering sensuality and sexuality

For many women who have suffered abuse and trauma, the body is *not* a safe place and they may have survived the pain by disconnecting or disassociating from their bodies. If that is the case, it necessary to work with a trauma-informed therapist who can assist with any intense fears or anxieties that may arise in trying to live in a more integrated, full-bodied way. In order to feel whole physically, spiritually and psychically, women need to feel safe and fully integrated into their bodies. I have found the previously referenced works of Peter Levine and somatic experiencing and Bessel Van Der Kolk's top-down, bottom-up approach to be particularly effective, however there are many approaches that might help with this process. In addition to therapy, practices such as yoga and massage are valuable for reconnecting with the body.

Sensuality is not necessarily about sexuality although it is, at its very root, desirable from a sexual perspective. While biologically, sex is typically the same: nakedness, stimulation of the body and orgasm, etc., sensuality is highly personal and a state of living and being. Connecting to one's physical body and senses is the process of living more sensually. Learning to tune in and pay attention to the *senses* (sight, smell, hearing, taste and touch) is a journey in itself. Two of the big problems with US culture in particular are that 1) the puritans really screwed us up and 2) when the 'sexual revolution' happened, we failed to include the sensual revolution with it. In our culture, sexuality and sexualization are *everywhere,* yet sensuality is left out. If we paid greater attention to our senses we would work, play and live very differently and we would definitely not engage in unconscious driven behaviors that feel harmful to our bodies.

When I half-jokingly say "the puritans screwed us up," I mean that the philosophical underpinnings of our culture distinctly assert that heaven is a true home and that we should deny the 'earthly' pleasures of the body and focus on the mind and spirit. This undercurrent is still alive in our culture. I remember distinctly being call "piggish" when I was a child for asking for a second helping of something I really enjoyed. I was also shamed at a middle school dance by an adult chaperone who thought I moved my hips and lower body too seductively. If you ask a French woman to say the first thing that comes to mind about a piece of chocolate cake, they will say "pleasure". Ask an American woman and we will say "guilt." I remember one of my teachers used to remind me that the first three letters of diet are die which explains the psychology of why diets fail a larger percentage of the time.

Where religions and philosophies left off, consumerism has taken its place. Feel bad about yourself? Buy this latest (fill in the blank) and you will feel better. The problem is that consumerism by its very design is made to make us feel empty again and again so that we will keep consuming.

The problem with denying our sensuality and even engaging in self-punishing behavior is that, at the deepest part of our being, we will eventually rebel. But many times we do so in very unbalanced and unhealthy ways. Developing the healthy feminine in us is about being open to receive pleasure.

We are integrated into our bodies by *feeling*. Because our psyches are trying to protect us from pain, especially if we have been traumatized or abused, we get frightened and shut ourselves down when we start to feel. This includes bodily sensations as well as emotions. Creating a practice of paying attention to all of our senses and enjoying the physical world around us is very transformative and healing. There are some exercises in the journal prompts at the end of the chapter to assist with this.

On our biological cycles:

As women, we must question the 'seeds' that have been planted in us about our own bodies and our gardens. Religions and cultural traditions that tell women that they are 'unclean' do great harm to our psyches. The medical profession as well has not only misinformed women about their own biological and psychological processes, particularly when it comes to sexuality, but has also propagated the idea that periods, pregnancy and childbirth are physical issues to cope with at best, and diseases to be treated at worst. In many indigenous cultures, women are viewed as sacred, holy and very powerful since we are most connected to spirit or God due to our theoretical ability bear children (whether we have physical children or not) as nurturers and givers-of-life. During menses (moontime) our power is viewed as so great that we can upset energies taking place in ceremonies so we sit outside the circles. Menstrual blood on cloth was given to warriors in some cultures to wear into battle for protection.

In many North American tribal traditions, women would do a moon lodge during menstruation and take four days off to rest, pray, meditate, do beadwork and generally rebalance themselves by allowing others to serve them and bring them food while they rested (I think we need to do this tradition today). I have always taught my daughter and the women I have worked with that they are most 'open' spiritually during that time of their cycle. Since we *are* more tuned in and open, I think the moodiness or irritability that we feel is for several reasons. During this time we are more attuned or tapped into the collective consciousness or soul wound of women in our ancestral line and also the larger female collective. Additionally, the relationships and issues in our lives are magnified during this time, particularly what is *not working*. So, rather than blaming our period, we need to pay close attention to what we are feeling during this time and the issues that trouble us the most. The issues are *real,* our cycles are just putting a spotlight and magnifying glass to them.

Pregnancy is another state in which women may be particularly sensitive and attuned and, in most indigenous cultures, there are ancient practices in place to keep women from harmful situations and states of mind. Women are believed to have an enormous spiritual impact on their unborn babies with both the obvious physical umbilicus and a spiritual one as well. Pregnancy and childbirth are important initiatory processes for women that are often ruined or disrupted by social and cultural practices that do not honor the feminine and the wisdom of the female body. For example, women since this beginning of time have given birth squatting or kneeling, working with the body and gravity to open the pelvis and make delivery easier on the laboring woman. The practice of lying on one's back to give birth was rumored to have been started by a voyeuristic Louis XIV; however, it was the physician François Mariceau who is credited with influencing the change in birthing position. As medicine became a profession, the male doctors needed to distinguish themselves as experts with skills and knowledge beyond humble profession of midwifery (which has existed since the beginning of time) and practices like episiotomies and scheduled C-sections often worked for the time and convenience and financial benefits of doctors, not a woman's natural body processes. Women are taught to fear their labors and birth processes and they give up total control of the process to others.

When I delivered my son, I was in my twenties and had read everything I could about the birthing process. I didn't have access to a midwife, so I waited as long as possible to go to the hospital so that I could labor with as much control over my labor process as possible. It was more than two and a half days, but I did lots of walking and bathing. I was in full labor when I got to the hospital (my mother was with me) and I heard a woman screaming in such a way that it terrified me. I asked the nurse if my labor was going to get worse and she said, "No, honey, you're already there". I still received a 10 centimeter episiotomy which was the *worst* part of the labor and completely unnecessary. Eight years later, when I had my daughter, I was much wiser. I sought out a midwife and had a water-birth, no drugs or medical intervention at all. It was a completely different experience. Of course, there are situations in which medical intervention is absolutely necessary for women and babies, but all too often, childbirth becomes medicalized in ways that disempower and frighten women, disconnecting us from our body-wisdom.

In many of the world's indigenous cultures, a woman in menopause is referred to as 'a woman who keeps her wisdom inside'. It is at this stage of life that a woman enters into the possibility of being an elder. I say 'possibility' here because, just as there are men in their 50s and beyond who, for whatever reason, have failed to be initiated into healthy manhood (and are psychically and spiritually still *boys)*, the same is true for women. If a woman is a healer or a medicine woman, she can give fully to the community now that she has raised her children. This is a stage of a woman's life that needs greater cultural understanding and celebrating. Women in contemporary Western cultures often profoundly grieve this phase of life and the loss of the mother inside them. The emphasis on beauty and youth often torments women in mid-life. For some women, however, this stage of life represents a new found liberation. Creating rituals to honor the complex spiritual, emotional and psychological transition for this stage of life eases the transition (see previous chapter).

Getting in touch with Body Wisdom

Did you ever have a friend who asked you for help and advice, yet she consistently ignored all of it? If you're like me, you probably gave up wasting time and energy trying to give her any advice or wisdom at all. Our relationships with our bodies can be a lot like that. Often we ignore the messages of our bodies and press on in very driven behaviors (I used to be the Queen of Driven Behavior). We ignore the instinctual messages that our body sends us and on top of all that, we can sometimes be very cruel and hateful towards different parts of our bodies. The more I have learned about psychology and the mind, the more I have learned about the wisdom of the body. For the last several hundred years (during the time paradoxically called the *enlightenment,* mentioned at the start of this chapter) science was born by separating from religion and 'superstition' and the mind was separated from the body. Today there is much movement toward the reintegration of science and spirituality and also the mind and the body. Mind is present in every cell of your body and we have only barely begun to understand the power of mind over matter.

As I am writing this chapter, I am doing a seasonal cleanse of my liver, gallbladder, bowel and skin (using herbs and hydrotherapies) guided by a detox specialist. As I detox, I am also amazed at the spiritual and psychological detox (releases) that happen. I have crazy dreams (which I track and journal of course) and my level of intuition and energy goes through the roof. As I have gained wisdom and greater connection with what my body needs, I also rest much more, engage in self-nurturing behaviors and stop myself much quicker when I return to the old well-worn, familiar role of Queen of Driven Behavior.

Reconnecting with the wisdom of our body starts with making peace with it and learning to love and accept it as the vehicle our soul is traveling in during this lifetime. Your body is an instrument of expression. Recognizing and consciously connecting with all parts and aspects of our body is not difficult, it just takes patience and practice.

Journal Prompts for the Keys of Body-Wisdom, Sex and Power

1. Think of your body and the center of your sexuality as a garden. Is it thriving? It is well-tended? Are there weeds there? Things you don't want to deal with or look at?

2. What is your relationship with your own body? Take time to journal on this relationship. Where are you loving and accepting? Where are you harsh or critical?

3. When you are harsh and critical of your body, where did those messages come from? How do those critical thoughts impact your energy or behavior?

4. In what ways can you become more loving and accepting to your physical body right now?

5. During the next 10 days, make it a practice to "check-in" with your physical body throughout your day. (You may need to set a reminder on your watch or phone.) What does your body need at this moment? To move and get up and stretch? To take a few deep breaths? Are you thirsty? Hungry? Or tired? Make a commitment to be a better listener to your body. Often the more we listen, the more it communicates!

6. Pay attention to physical sensations, especially those that are pleasurable. Using all of your senses can reawaken your connection and integration into your body. Dedicate a day to pay close attention to one sense at a time.

Reawakening the senses:

Day 1: dedicate the day to all of your skin sensations. The skin is the largest organ in the body and filled with energy and sensation all day long that we typically only pay attention to when something feels uncomfortable. Feel your skin in all different places. What textures (e.g. your pillowcase or soft clothing) or things feel good (e.g. how does the water or special soap in your shower feel? Pay attention to touch, both giving and receiving. What touch or skin sensations delight you and give you pleasure? Journal your day's experiences.

Day 2: dedicate the day to hearing. Notice as many sounds as you can throughout the day. Try keeping a list for a day of all the sounds you notice. We block out many sounds around us so that we can focus and pay attention to other things. What sounds are pleasing to your ears?

Day 3: dedicate the day to taste. Really deliberately taste everything thing you are eating and drinking. Try to notice as many different aspects of taste that you can. What tastes give you pleasure?

Day 4: dedicate the day to your sense of smell. Smell is a very primal sense and is well-developed at birth. We are typically unaware of much of the information coming through our sense of smell. Journal all the smells you noticed throughout the day (good and bad!)

Day 5: dedicate the day to vision. Try and notice as many details as you can in your visual environment. What sights delight you or give you pleasure? Journal what you notice.

🔑🔑🔑

The Keys:
Mentors and Allies

*"Social ties are
the cheapest medicine we have."*
--S.E. Taylor

Two decades ago, psychologist Dr. Shelley E. Taylor wrote The *Tending Instinct*[17] as well as hundreds of articles and papers on women's previously unrecognized responses to stress. It turned out that the classic theories about stress responses (fight, flight or freeze) missed a crucial and hardwired biological difference between women and men. Taylor and her colleagues revolutionized our understanding of human behavior in finding that we are biologically programmed to care for one another. Taylor calls this response the *tend and befriend* or the *tending instinct*. In times of trouble, fear or great stress, instead of running or fighting people, we are biologically programmed to care for one another and turn to the social group to both give and receive social support.

This nurturing instinct is hardwired into our genes, in our brain chemistry, in our hormones and in our reactions to the world around us. Tending instinct is as natural as other

---

17. Taylor, S. E. (2002). *The tending instinct: How nurturing is essential to who we are and how we live.* Macmillan.

behaviors, such as the search for food or sleeping. Taylor and her colleagues assert that tending instinct is essential for ensuring long and healthy lives. She explains what drives women to seek one another's company and tend to the young and the infirm. This can often provide great benefit to the group but, if unbalanced, can come at a great cost to the individual (as explored previously in the chapter on Relationship Cages). Now twenty years later, we broadly recognize the ways in which the lack of parental tending during childhood can craft the biology or trajectory in children toward mental or physical illnesses. There are also a number of theories on how women's tendency to tend and befriend as a reaction to stress may help us not only live longer but also better cope with losses such as divorce or the death of a loved one.

My point here is that reaching out to supportive friends mentors and allies is a *key* strategy with lots of biological evolutionary 'evidence' for our mental and physical health through stressful change and transition. Mentors and allies are also essential in assisting with our spiritual and psychological growth and expansion.

On Mentors

There is a poem by an unknown author about friendship 'for a reason, for a season and for a lifetime'. It explores the idea that some people come into our lives for a specific reason; we've called out (most often unconsciously) for someone to teach us something specifically to further our soul's growth and development. Some people come for a season of our lives but the relationship fades away with the next season. Lifetime relationships are exactly that. They can wax and wane like the cycles of the moon but are constant throughout our lifespan. I believe that mentoring relationships are also *for a reason, for a season* and *for a lifetime.* Relationships with mentors are critical for our growth and development, but they can often become detrimental if not minded with care and a high degree of spiritual awareness.

It is important here to talk first about what mentoring *is not*. Mentors are typically older, more experienced individuals or more advanced in a knowledge area we are seeking. As *authorities,* we need to use caution to not unconsciously project our issues with our first authority figures (our parents or the people who raised us) onto our mentors. This means knowing what your issues are (no one comes through childhood unscathed in some way), owning them and bringing your whole adult self and self-responsibility into the mentor relationship. This does not mean that past relationship triggers won't arise (such as abandonment or self-worth, etc...); you will just 'catch' them before they contaminate the mentor relationship. The same applies to the mentors you choose. If I am asserting or advocating what is best for me and my mentor tells me I am acting like a petulant child, I'm out of there! I've known many women who are so starved for parental approval and attention from their past that they engage in mentoring relationships that become controlling and harmful to their growth and development.

So, parent/family of origin issues aside, mentors are important people who have blazed the trails you are seeking to head down and they can be invaluable guides on your journey. You can learn from their experiences, avoid pitfalls and also gain much perspective and wisdom. The *best* mentors embody or model the characteristics you need to step into the shoes you are creating for yourself. The best mentors have the perfect balance of honesty and compassion, directness and the willingness to leave things open-ended for you to discover your own answers. Mentors can often see gifts and parts of ourselves that we have not yet recognized, and they tell us so. A quality mentor will *not* require an extended commitment or unreasonable demands on your time, energy and resources. Watch your mentors carefully with a critical eye. If they appear to not be practicing what they are preaching, this is a giant red-flag. I also look at the other people the mentor is attracting and working with. Are they moving forward? Are they stuck in the same loops and patterns year after year? This is problematic. Good mentors call us out when we are going back to sleep. They hold us accountable to changes. While there will always be those folks who stay stuck no matter what (as a therapist, this is my most frustrating situation), there should be 'shooting stars': people who you can see make and sustain dramatic change in their lives.

In leaving my very unhappy and destructive marriages, I had *several* mentors over the years it took to finally sever the ties and move on to freedom. 1) A therapist who had a long relationship with me and my family (I told him in a therapy session with her), 2) an older couple who were therapists focusing on astrology and karmic relationships and their meanings and 3) an older, strong masculine mentor who shepherded me step-by-step through each stage of breaking free. Even though I had a Ph.D. in psychology and years of clinical experience, I needed these mentors to help me see what I was blind to. I recall the older couple asking me to put my 'clinician hat' on and see my soon-to-be ex-husband through those eyes. It was like getting hit with a wall of bricks. I finally saw him for who he really was and was able to really get clear on my need to get free and release any hope of salvaging the marriage. They helped me to understand that the guilt I was experiencing was contaminated energy from the past (not this lifetime) and that my karmic reason for our relationship was now completed and over. My older male mentor helped me to recognize healthy masculine versus the collapsed unhealthy masculine and understand that ways in which being with a collapsed, angry man-child had become my cage.

When you are searching for a mentor, be clear about what you are seeking and why. My most recent mentor came to me through an intuition when meditating; my inner voice said *"work with her."* Some of my past mentors appeared in my dreams as teachers and I sought them out in my waking life.

I have found that gender does matter for me. Currently I am working on embodying the sacred feminine in my work life. Clearly, I need women who are further along in mastery to assist me in this.

You need to know when a mentoring relationship has served its purpose. I tend to stay too long. I've had several mentors with whom I stay in contact and they continue to be a part of my life, just not at the level of intensity we had during the active mentoring relationship. At my age, I have had many of my mentors pass on. I call them in during ceremonies and during my mediations and I do feel the energy of those relationships, even though their bodies are long gone.

Leaving a mentoring relationship can be hard. If you are honest, grateful and respectful in letting the mentor know you've received what you came for and needed and are now moving on, the *only* acceptable response is them wishing you well and on your way.

True mentors are honest, have our backs and model the aspects and characteristics we are seeking to cultivate within ourselves. Find mentors in your therapists, coaches or teachers. The most highly evolved women I know have great therapists or mentors. My Indian father had a saying: "Arieahn, your eyebrow is one inch from your eye, but you need a mirror to see it!" Let the mentor be your mirror.

On allies

Allies are also important keys to change. They can be a bit different than mentors because their role and function are to *align* with us. Allies hold our light for us until we can pick it back up. They know our songs and remember them until we can sing them again. They remind us that we are beautiful and awesome and not to listen to the self-critic inside of us or judge ourselves by the number on the scale or the "flaws" we think we see in the mirror. They are our tribe, our close friends and family who unconditionally 'get us.' We need them to *just listen* and be on our side. This week, while working on this chapter, I mistakenly reached out to male friend in my life to vent about something. True to masculine form, he sprang into action mode and tried to fix the situation--in effect making things much worse. I hear about this dilemma and dynamic all the time from my female clients and girlfriends. We often need to remember which allies are good for what we need in the moment. My life-long friend Julie, who I've known since high school, has this amazing gift of seeing things from a higher, more balanced perspective. I can always count on her to gently help me see multiple sides of a situation without feeling like she is judging me for my feelings. Another example of specific allies is my sister Nikki. She comes from the school of "get over yourself, you namby pamby" (we laugh about this frequently) so I know she may or not give me a sympathetic ear if I need one, but I can always count on her to tell me to "get over myself" just when I need to hear that.

One of my current clients is a full-time professional and the mom of a young daughter with a husband who travels a lot. She moved recently and has realized the need for social connections so she reached out and found a group of women (other working moms in her town) she calls her *mom tribe*. This is so essential in our lives and our spiritual and psychological health.

The literature on resilience shows that social isolation is *not* a resilience strategy. Men in our culture, however, tend to either fight, flee or crawl into their caves and self-isolate when they are super stressed or wounded. Women who are high-achieving in masculine energy or in high masculine energy settings, often co-opt this pattern to their detriment. Women who have been wounded by other women who are unhealthy, overly competitive or toxic have good reason to avoid other women. This, however, is a mistake in that we are then missing vital sources for support and connection. I would encourage these women to keep searching for good women allies. They are out there. Don't stop looking.

It is critical that we are self-aware in these relationships. We need to attend to good boundaries and expectations and make sure we aren't overly dependent or too heavily relying on our allies in such a way that we burn them out. This is a sure-fire way to ruin and end a friendship.

Being a mentor and an ally

Tending instinct is reaching out *for* support and nurturing, as well as giving it to others. In the true feminine spirit of reciprocity, we give back and consciously serve as mentors and allies to those in our lives. It is most gratifying to know that you have made a life-changing difference in someone's life, whether or not you are a "formal" helper (e.g. therapist or healer) or not. There are biological, spiritual and psychological gifts and benefits when we serve and tend to others. When you are a mentor or an ally to someone, you are always self-checking to make sure you are not creating codependence or over-giving to both your own detriment and to the stunting of the self-sufficiency and evolution of the person you are working with. Paying attention to our energy when we are working with someone in this capacity is *key*. Do you leave the exchange energized and optimistic or drained or depressed? Your energy and emotions have valuable messages about what is going on in the spiritual and unconscious processes.

Similar to mentors, allies can serve different functions of support in a multitude of ways. To come full circle to where this chapter began, tending instinct, and reaching *to nurture* as well as *to receive* nurturing as a response to stress, is biologically and evolutionarily hardwired in our brains. Some of our mentors and allies are for specific reasons, some for certain seasons and others will remain throughout our lives.

Journal Prompts on Mentors and Allies

1. What is an area of your life where you could really use a mentor?

2. How do you imagine that this mentor can help you?

3. What are the specific qualities or gifts you are looking for in a mentor?

4. What are you willing and able to bring into the mentoring relationship?

5. Are you coachable?

🗝🗝🗝

The Keys:
Connecting to Nature
Rebalancing & Recharging

"Thousands of tired, nerve-shaken, over-civilized people are beginning to find out that going to the mountains is going home; that wilderness is a necessity; and that mountain parks and reservations are useful not only as fountains of timber and irrigating rivers, but as fountains of life." --John Muir, 1901

When I was struggling to complete my dissertation, I was typing on my patio and hummingbirds came to drink my red and purple salvia. I was stunned and delighted as I had never seen hummingbirds at that time of year or at the house where I was living. I looked up the symbol of hummingbirds across cultures and traditions. There were a number of qualities such as joy and lightness of being, but one source really stood out for me. It said that hummingbirds symbolize completion of the impossible. I then remembered that six years earlier, when I began my Ph.D., a graduate mentor had given me a crystal hummingbird for my desk. When I completed my dissertation and flew to Santa Barbara for my defense, in the hotel room bathroom was (you guessed it) a painting of a hummingbird.

Upon completion of my Ph.D. people gave me gifts and items with hummingbirds on them. (I hadn't said anything to any of them). During this particular part of my journey, hummingbirds were important helpers and allies.

My crystal hummingbird from graduate school

In the earlier chapter on instinct-injury, I briefly explored our connection to animals (in my case, horses) as lifelong important spiritual teachers and allies for my life and work. I encourage women in times of challenge and transition to get in touch with the energies and strengths of the animals they feel drawn to. It is important to pay attention to the animals that come to us in dreams and also present themselves in our waking lives. Women have always been deeply connected and intertwined with nature and the natural world. Due to our biological rhythms, divine feminine energy, potential capacity to give birth or nuture young that may or may not be our own, we can't help but feel connections, even if we live over-civilized modern lives that make connecting with nature difficult.

One of the important keys and ways to heal, re-balance and regain our energy is to make a conscious effort to spend time in nature and connect with the natural world. This doesn't have to mean expensive trips or moving, just finding creative ways to spend quality time in nature. One of my Native Elders used to say that a person could not be considered healthy without spending a *minimum* of an hour a day outside. Many women don't have any real time in nature, especially if we live and work in urban environments where we go from a home to a car to an office and then back again. This is especially true in climates that have seasonal weather challenges. Part of that is cultural as well. When I traveled to Denmark and Sweden, they shared a saying: "there is no bad weather, just bad dressers." The people make a point of dressing appropriately for the weather and not letting weather deter them from spending quality time outside. This was an important reminder for me as well. When I lived in an urban setting, having dogs to walk helped because I needed to take them for potty and exercise every day.

Now that I live on a farm, I spend a great deal of time each day outside and I believe this has really made a difference in my energy and ability to balance mentally and emotionally demanding work. Even with farm life, I still make a conscious efforts to take walks in nature and ground myself as a healing salve. Since I have lived here, I've hosted a number of retreats and it continues to amaze me that people are so impacted by their time on my land. I have to resist the temptation to give them too much "content" and remember that often it is the quiet time on the land that participants need most.

Nature Vigils

Indigenous people around the world and our all of our ancestors understood the healing power of spending time alone in nature. Numerous rites of passage and ceremonies involve connecting with the natural world as a means for healing and visioning. I have participated, co-led and hosted nature vigils (or retreats) for psychological and spiritual benefits for the last two decades. Taking a full day or several days in nature has a number of powerful benefits to the mind, body and spirit.

Western science and psychology is now confirming the wisdom that many cultures have known all along: the Elder who suggested that we needed at least an hour a day outside was right on target.

A team study of 20,000 people, led by Mathew White of the European Centre for Environment & Human Health at the University of Exeter, found that people who spent two hours a week in green spaces (local parks or other natural environments), either all at once or spaced over several visits, were substantially more likely to report good health and psychological well-being than those who didn't. Two hours was a hard boundary; the study showed no benefit for those who did meet that threshold.[18]

Research has also shown the medical benefits of even just viewing nature scenes. In studies of hospitalized patients, those exposed to nature scenes had their brains light up in the regions of the brain linked with empathy and love. These patients showed a better tolerance for pain, a greater ability to overcome adverse affects and less time being hospitalized. Being *in* nature has shown evidence of reduced blood pressure, stabilized heart rates and a decrease in stress hormones.

In the field of Western psychology, my suggestion that nature is "grounding" and healing sounded woo-woo twenty years ago, however, there are now twenty years of medical studies on the earth's electromagnetic frequency, known as the Schumann Resonance. The earth pulses out this frequency and the human body is fully conductive. Every cell in our bodies becomes immediately grounded whenever we touch the earth directly. The medical studies indicate that when we

---

18. White, M.P., Alcock, I., Grellier, J. *et al*. Spending at least 120 minutes a week in nature is associated with good health and wellbeing. *Sci Rep* 9, 7730 (2019). https://doi.org/10.1038/s41598-019-44097-3

are connected to the earth's energy, our bodies naturally go into a healing state. Everything from our brainwaves to our muscle tension to our heartbeat responds to this energy.[19] The good news is that the positive physical and psychological benefits of grounding are immediate.

We are genetically programmed to connect with the natural world and find trees, plants, water and nature elements engaging. Being in nature allows us to use our five senses and provides relief and respite from an overactive mind. Living in busy urban or suburban centers can be exhausting. The impact of too much screen time and technology has created what some refer to as *nature deficit disorder* or *nature deprivation*. These conditions have been linked to greater levels of anxiety and depression in children, adolescents and adults. The Schumann frequency is 7.83 Hz which is the same range as alpha and theta brain waves. There is ongoing research on the ability of this frequency to influence DNA. The wave frequency at which the human cavity resonates is between 6 and 8 hertz. All biological systems operate in this same frequency range. There is ongoing research that also indicates that higher frequencies (16-60 Hz) are harmful to the mind and body in a number of ways. Certainly all of the wave and frequencies of modern technology are something we've only recently had to cope with for our balance, health and well-being.

---

19. Sifferlin, A. (2016). The healing power of nature. *Time Mag, 188*, 24-26.

In his book *Forest Bathing: How Trees Can Help You Find Health and Happiness*, Dr. Qing Li explores the sensory power of walking (not bathing in the Western sense of the word) and immersing ourselves in the sensory experience of a forest as a means for greater health and mental well-being. Since connecting with the earth allows us to access our alpha waves more easily, the relaxation, recharging and refocusing can assist with our exhausted minds. When spending time in nature, we slow down enough for the 'healing' to catch us.

Me and my sister Nikki literally "tree-hugging" on a hike in Muir Woods (2016)

Water, the seaside and the "blue–mind"

Throughout my adult life I have tracked the most powerful and spiritually transformative experiences to those at the ocean. (For example, the seaside ritual in the section "How to Use This Book"). I started my initiation into my soul's purpose ("I'll do whatever it takes") on the beach on the Pacific Ocean in Ixtapa. My graduate study in Santa Barbara allowed me lots of time walking along the beach contemplating my education, my relationships and my life's path. I let go of my spiritual contracts with both fathers of my children, as well as my mother's soul-pattern/legacy in rituals I created at the Gulf of Mexico.

My teachers took this after I released some ritual ashes and a stone into the Gulf of Mexico (2016)

More recently, in 2017, 2018 and 2022, the beaches in Nosara, Nicoya, Costa Rica have been spiritual rejuvenation high points for me. I have always felt a very powerful attraction to water and especially to oceans. In researching the mental and spiritual benefits of being near them, I now know why. Similarly to the studies on nature and healing, there are a number of studies indicating that proximity to oceans, breathing in ocean air, as well as being *in* the ocean has a number of positive psychological and physical benefits. Even in ancient times, the Greeks recognized what they termed the "water cure"; many of the practices are still part of healing in many cultures of the world.

Pictures from Costa Rica (2017, 2018 and 2022)

In his bestselling book, *Blue Mind: The Surprising Science That Shows How Being Near, In, On, or Under Water Can Make You Happier, Healthier, More Connected, and Better at What You Do*, marine biologist Wallace J. Nichols focuses on the proven scientific evidence that being close to bodies of water promotes mental health and happiness. He uses the term "blue mind" to describe the mildly meditative state we fall into when near, in, on or under water. It's the antidote to what we refer to as "red mind," which is the anxious, over-connected and over-stimulated state that defines the new normal of modern life. Research has proven that spending time near the water is essential to achieving an elevated and sustained happiness.

Nichols emphasizes that the blue mind doesn't need to come from the ocean:

> *"Most of us have access to water, lakes or oceans in some form -- and we underutilize their potential. Whether it's a deeply relaxing vacation or a week-end getaway, water is the best way to reset. There are many locations that you can go to experience a blue mind -- you don't necessarily need to be near the ocean. If you look at a map of the U.S. or world, there is blue everywhere -- rivers, lakes, ponds -- and not to mention pools and what we call "domesticated water." You don't have to go far. "Blue mind" is not an exclusively ocean-only conversation, it's a water*

*conversation, and there are incredibly amazing wa-
terways everywhere -- around the world."*

On gardening: the magic of seeds

At the start of the Covid-19 pandemic, as I was working on
this book, there was a run on seeds and gardening supplies
(as well as toilet paper, which I totally do not understand).
I, too, got caught up in this internal drive/desire and spent
quite a bit of time creating a "moon garden" on my urban
patio. I believe this desire for seeds and gardens was coming
from our urgent need for hope and healing, drawing on our
deepest collective wisdom. Gardening grounds us and it gives
us something to look forward to. In seeds and gardens, we
can grow and see evidence of hope. Since the beginning of
human civilization, we have recognized and revered seeds
for the gift of life they represent. We have a long history of
legends, myths and fairy tales on the magic power of seeds,
and religious traditions around the world recognize seeds as
powerful tiny life-potential. Some traditions have taboos and
guidelines about how seeds should be handled and used. The
pomegranate with its multiple seeds is important in a number
of traditions, including for the ancient Greeks. Earth-based
traditions consecrated seeds in ceremony and ritual. (In my
Winter Solstice celebrations, we bless and put the energy of
intention for the Spring and year ahead into seeds).

Dr. Sue Stuart-Smith is a psychiatrist and author of the recent book *The Well-Gardened Mind: The Restorative Power of Nature.* She believes that gardening is a form of space-time medicine, an idea that Larry Dossey proposed in the 1980s. In her book, Stuart-Smith describes the healing effects on prison inmates and soldiers with PTSD engaged in horticultural programs, as well as patients suffering from grief and depression. She reminds the reader that this is the lasting imprint of our hunter gatherer evolutionary past. Gardening is a very accessible form of creativity. It allows us to create something new. There *is* a balance, however, that needs to be struck with gardening between being and doing. We don't need more housework--in this case, outdoor housework. In my first Spring season living on my farm people asked me if I was going to garden and I thought, "Are you kidding me?" I felt so overwhelmed by the new level of work with stalls and horses that it seemed impossible and impractical to add this to my life. I am committed step-by-step and over time to add this to my tools for healing and balance.

The power of this key of connection to nature for rebalancing and healing is that it doesn't have to cost anything except finding green spaces and committing to the time to experience grounding and nature on a regular (weekly) basis. The more exhausted and depleted you are, the more time you should spend in nature rebalancing and recharging yourself.

Journal Prompts for Connecting to Nature

1. Think back to when you were very young. What are your memories of experiences in nature?

2. What animals or creatures were you most drawn to and fascinated by?

3. Was there a point in your life where you found nature to be healing or rebalancing ?

4. Was there a point in your life when you lost your connection to nature? What happened exactly? How did this impact you?

5. List several practices or ways to reconnect with nature in your life now. What is the healing or rebalancing you are seeking? What can you commit to for your health and well-being?

🗝🗝🗝

Being
a
Chatelaine

"True nobility is not being better than someone else.
It is about being better than you used to be ... stay
focused on growth with constant awareness."
Dr. Wayne W. Dyer[20]

Together we have gone on a journey of self-discovery, transition and change. The goal of this self-work is transcending an ordinary life and diving into an extraordinary one. This takes patience, bravery, honesty, faith and risk. Only the strongest women undertake this path to become the chatelaine in their own lives. We keep walking the path, refining our abilities, tools and awareness and seeking to experience joy on every part of the journey.

Below I have cultivated a list of qualities and guiding principles that enable a woman to truly be the chatelaine in her own life. These are *all* important and not in any rank order.

Qualities of a Chatelaine

1. Self-aware, embraces all of her feelings, is deeply self-reflective

2. Guided by intuition and her vision

3. Strong-willed and level-headed

---

20. Dyer, W. W. (2010). *The power of intention: Learning to co-create your world your way.* Hay House, Inc. p 84

4. Focused and intentional with attention, energy and all resources

5. Open-minded, clear about desires and opinions but not rigid or closed off   to others

6. Clear boundaries, faithful to herself and her vision

7. Aware of strengths and areas for development

8. Empathic

9. Views time as an invaluable resource, will not waste hers or anyone else's

10. Never co-dependent

11. Kind and compassionate

12. Courageous and adventurous

13. Self-loving and committed to enlightened self-interest

As we explored throughout this book, self-awareness and self-knowledge are of utmost importance. The process of accessing emotions and understanding self succeeds through a deliberate journal practice and a willingness to be open and truthful with ourselves. Working with a skilled therapist, coach or spiritual mentor can also aid in this quality. Quiet, reflective time and accessing and trusting intuition are essential for visioning the life and changes that you want to make. Being strong-willed and level-headed requires a willingness to trust your intuition and vision, as well as knowing how to stablize and ground your emotional energy. Connected to this is knowing how to recharge your energy when it has been depleted.

To be focused and intentional means that your priorities are clear because they align with your vision for your life. Knowing that resources and time are needed to execute your vision means that you will use them wisely and not waste them on things, people and situations that are not in alignment with your life-vision. I would include here that this also means paying close attention to what you feed your mind and what you give your attention to. There is so much junk and garbage vying for our attention, particularly in media, we must be judicious about what we "mind." This is where crystal clear boundaries and being faithful and dedicated to your own life are essential.

We need to retain our kindness, empathy and compassion without losing ourselves in the process. As women we must have a high-degree of awareness of our tendency and deep imprinted learning to be overly "other" centered or to over-give. An antidote to this is focusing on self-compassion *first*.

And finally, a Chatelaine must be courageous and adventurous. Visioning an extraordinary life and being willing to take bold (and sometimes messy) action to execute it takes courage and also the spirit of adventure and trusting one's North Star.

Detailing the Vision

In the very first section, *Start with a Vision,* the suggested meditation started with finding a symbol for growth and transformation, assuming that there may have been, at that time in your process and journey, the need for recognizing your current traps and cages, the need for gathering strength and energy and reclaiming your power, the need for releasing what no longer served you (clearing the hearth) and the need to find or re-spark passion. At this point, having done much of this work together, you can ask and begin to expect a more detailed vision for your life.

Beyond the North Star... Your Detailed Vision

To prepare for this exercise, find a quite place where you will not be disturbed for at least 20 minutes. Have a journal and pen handy to take notes (or draw) and find a comfortable place to sit or lie down where you will not have to think about your body. (If your body is uncomfortable, you will find it very difficult to quiet and focus your mind).

This exercise is a guided imagery meditation. My suggestion is that you read it aloud in your own voice and record it to play it back. You can also access a recording of this on my website at: www.drarieahnmb.com

Beyond your North Star Vision

Put your body in a place where you are comfortable and don't have to think about it. You can lie down on your back or sit with your back resting and your feet flat to the floor. Close your eyes softly. Start with some slow rhythmic deep breaths. Don't work to take the breath in, just fill completely and exhale completely with ease. Breathe in relaxation and breathe out tension. Allow your body to progressively relax. Start with your face: relax your forehead and the tiny muscles around your eyes and let that relaxation spread like a wave all the way to the soles of your feet. Relax your jaw and loosen your tongue from the roof of your mouth.

Take another breath and, as you exhale, let your shoulders drop. Feel the upper arm relax, then the lower arm and then your hands. Extend your fingers out. Breathe in and then, on the exhale, wiggle your fingers slightly and let go of any tension you were holding. Relax your back body and let it be supported. Relax your abdomen, then your upper legs then lower legs. Feel your feet. Wiggle your toes slightly and let go of any tension you are holding.

Allow yourself to feel totally relaxed and at ease. Whenever you relax like this you receive great benefit to your mind, body and spirit and this is so.

You have a mind and your mind is important to you. It holds all of your memories, knowledge and experience. You have a mind but you are so much more than that.

You have a body and your body is important to you. You can be still or in movement, hungry or full, tired or energized, tense or relaxed. Your body can change and be many things but you are so much more than just your physical body.

You have emotions and feelings. They can change in a moment; your feelings are important indicators to your level of alignment with who you truly are. They are important to you but you are much more than your emotions, your body or your mind. You are a point of consciousness- a soul. The true you has always existed before you were in this physical body having your experiences of this life... before you had the memories, knowledge and emotions you've gained while on your physical trail. Acknowledge and feel this ancient energy of the true you. Let your facial expression, breathing and posture reflect this blended energy of your personality/identity in this current lifetime with the true eternal you--your true-self within you.

When you decided to come into this life, you had a goal or mission. There were things you wanted to accomplish and things you wanted to learn and contribute to the world. You can call this your higher-purpose or your soul's purpose. In the process of becoming who you are right now, you may have forgotten these things or perhaps got a little side-tracked. That's okay. You've learned much already and everything has prepared you in some way for your purpose, even if it was not clear until this moment.

You received a symbol a while back to use as a North Star to hold in your mind to guide you to this work and this transformation. Picture this symbol now in your mind's-eye.

Take a full breath in and imagine you are drawing energy from deep in the core of the earth through the soles of your feet. Let that beautiful, balanced, slow energy light up all the cells in your body from your feet, up to your legs, your torso, up to your heart, your throat, your forehead and then up and out the crown of your head. Imagine a beautiful golden ball of light surrounding you. Take another full, deep breath. Now imagine the things you want to have, be and do in your life right now. Where and how do you want to live? Picture it now. How do you want to feel? Breathe in and feel that way now. What are the goals you want to accomplish? See yourself completing those goals now. How will you use your knowledge, gifts and talents? How will this serve others and the world? Take a moment and play a movie in your minds-eye of you being, doing and having the things that your heart desires most. Get all of your senses involved too, sound, smell, feeling. Enjoy the vision. It feels so good to allow our minds and spirit to connect with this.You can send light and energy to this vision whenever you are discouraged or need inspiration and this is so. You can come back to this vision in your relaxed meditative state at any time to add and edit the vision's details.

Give gratitude for this time, connection and vision and, when you are ready, flutter your eyes open and return to the room. Be sure to take any notes you want to remember in your journal.

Staying in focused alignment

The work of the chatelaine is never done. We continually revision and refocus at every stage of life. We are willing to let go of old dreams and visions and embrace new ones as we evolve. This is the process of our soul's evolution. We continually strive to be better and better each day in all aspects of our lives. Excellence, not perfection, and compassion, especially self-compassion, are the hallmarks of our lives. We are human, we falter, we resurrect old patterns that we thought were long gone. We learn lessons again that we thought we had mastered, only this time on a deeper level. Even as I write this, I found myself last weekend in a pattern of over-giving and appeasement where I was feeling tension in my belly and giving my power away. I heard a voice remind me: "Do not give your power away, to anyone, in any circumstance, for any reason," and I immediately course-corrected my behaviors. I found myself at the completion of this book, during the editing process, in a relationship cage with someone who was not who they pretended to be. It was, in many ways, an opportunity Spirit gave me to 'field test' my own process in this book in a very short period of time. Journaling, not surprisingly, was really a key here. I could trace all of the entries where I had niggling tiny doubts in the way back of my awareness, where I wrote that something 'felt off' even if I couldn't identify it concretely right away. It confirmed and helped me to see a pattern and, as things escalated and I was being called unstable or crazy, there everything was in my own writing. It confirmed without any doubt that I needed to exit. This happened in a matter of a few short months rather than *years* as it had in my past. I am so grateful for this lesson.

But we learn and *know* how to use the keys and return to them again and again and perfect our own individual processes. We trust that we can always return to alignment. We trust that we can and will recognize cages before the doors slam and we get stuck. If for some reason we find ourselves in a cage, we can get out much more quickly because we *know* in our hearts and souls that we have the keys.

Staying in focused alignment and journeying toward our life-vision is a day-by-day practice. The things that are most helpful are 1) taking care of the body, 2) taking care of the spirit and mind and 3) reminding ourselves daily about what is most important to us.

Taking care of our bodies is common sense. *Listening* and honoring the needs of the body for good nutrition, exercise/ movement, relaxation, time in nature and grounding every day should be non-negotiable practices of self-care in our lives. Feed your mind and your body healthy things. Taking care of our spirit and minds can be any form of self-reflection (such as journaling), learning new things and dedicating ourselves to a spiritual practice of prayer or meditation. Reminding ourselves every day about what is most important to us is essential, as well as a regular gratitude practice.

The journal questions below are some suggestions tracking for your practices:

Morning Ritual:

....

....

....

Last night I went to bed at :
This morning I slept until :

My morning ritual will include:

1)

2)

3)

The most important thing I need to accomplish today is:

....

....

....

Today, I am most looking forward to:

....

....

....

How can I make today GREAT or AMAZING?

Tonight I will go to bed at:

Tomorrow I will sleep until:

Evening Ritual- (At the end of the day, relaxation is essential. I highly recommend NOT watching the news at night or things that are negative or upsetting. Also dim your lights and avoid blue light from computers, tablets and phones after 8p.m.)

My evening ritual will include:

1)

2)

3)

The three things I am most grateful for today are:

1)

2)

3)

Final Words

This is by far the most difficult section to write. As I have written this book over many months, I was imagining a conversation with you--the reader. I could picture you and feel you and I tried to anticipate where your pain points, confusion or questions might be. I hoped that you were getting my sense of humor in the places where I tried to share it. I imagined what you might say about the journaling exercises or other stories. I wondered where your attention was held and where it wandered. Maybe because I've been a therapist/healer and teacher for so long, writing this felt like a *relationship*.

As I wrote in the chapter *Keys of Mentoring and Allies*, these relationships are for a reason, or a season or a lifetime. Our season is coming to a close. The reason for you taking this journey with me was, I hope, finding a path and a process for transformation and change that enables you to move from ordinary to extraordinary in your vision for your life. It is my sincere hope and prayer that this book guided you in making changes and improvements in your life, your relationships and, most importantly, within your self. To the chatelaine in you.

Some Recommended Reading

Below is a list of some of my favorite books - both new and old... for more books visit my social media and website *www.drarieahnmb.com*

Bolen, J. S., & Steinem, G. (1984). *Goddesses in everywoman: A new psychology of women* (p. 334). New York: Harper & Row.

Brown, B. (2012). *The Power of Vulnerability: Teachings on Authenticity, Connection and.*

Choquette, S. (2008). *The Time Has Come# to Accept Your Intuitive Gifts!*. Hay House, Inc.

Choquette, S. (2011). *Your Heart's Desire: Instructions for Creating the Life You Really Want.* Hay House, Inc.

Estes, C. P. (1995). *Women who run with the wolves: Myths and stories of the wild woman archetype.* Ballantine Books.

Hicks, E., & Hicks, J. (2004). *Ask and it is given: Learning to manifest your desires.* Hay House, Inc.

Honda, K. (2019). *Happy Money: The Japanese Art of Making Peace with Your Money.* Simon and Schuster.

Levine, P. A. (1997). *Waking the tiger: Healing trauma: The innate capacity to transform overwhelming experiences.* North Atlantic Books.

Perel, E. (2007). *Mating in captivity: Unlocking erotic intelligence* (p. 272). New York, NY: Harper.

Stevens, D. D., & Cooper, J. E. (2020). *Journal keeping: How to use reflective writing for learning, teaching, professional insight and positive change*. Stylus Publishing, LLC.

Vanderkam, L. (2017). *I know how she does it: How successful women make the most of their time*. Penguin.

Vanderkam, L (2019). *Juliet's School of Possibilities: A little story about the power of priorities*. .

🗝🗝🗝